Running a Nurture Group

Simon Bishop

SAGE

Los Angeles • London • New Delhi • Singapore

SAGE Publications Ltd
1 Olivers's Yard
55 City Road
London EC1Y 1SP

SAGE Publications Inc
2455 Teller Road
Thousand Oaks, California 91320

SAGE Publications India Pvt Ltd
B 1/I 1 Mohan Cooperative Industrial Area
Mathura Road,
New Delhi 110 044

SAGE Publications Asia-Pacific Pte Ltd
33 Pekin Street #02-01
Far East Square
Singapore 048763

Library of Congress Control Number: 2008921642

British Library Cataloguing in Publication Data
A catalogue record for this book is available from the British Library

ISBN 978-1-4129-3526-5
ISBN 978-1-4129-3527-2 (pbk)

Typeset by Bookcraft Ltd, Stroud, Gloucestershire
Printed in Great Britain by The Cromwell Press Ltd,
Trowbridge, Wiltshire
Printed on paper from sustainable resources

Contents

Acknowledgements

This book would not have been written without the support of my wife Sarah and my daughters, Maisie and Eliza. All my love and a big thank-you go to them for inspiration, help, patience and advice.

Thanks to Mum and Dad and all the family for encouragement.

Thanks to Sarah Bullmore and Carole Whittard at Christ Church First School, Frome, for vision and effort in making the nurture group a reality.

A big thank-you also to all the dedicated staff of Christ Church First School, with special thanks to Claire Harrington and Liz Penney for all your hard work over the years.

About the Author

Simon Bishop is married with two daughters and lives in Somerset. He has taught for over twenty years in Primary and First schools. Six years ago he set up a full-time 'Boxall model' nurture group that he currently runs. The inspiration for the nurture group came from an article in the *Special Needs Information Press* (www.snip-newsletter. co.uk). Simon started to use an assessment tool called the Boxall Profile which helped him to begin to understand more fully why some children find school such a difficult place to be, and would benefit from being in a nurture group. He continues to be inspired by the principles of nurture groups, and how this intervention enables the school to adjust to meet the needs of the children who can't meet the needs of the school. He also finds that nurture groups enable adults at school to respond to children with greater empathy and understanding.

How to Use the CD-Rom

The CD-Rom contains pdf files of resources from the book separated by chapter. You will need Acrobat Reader version 3 or higher to view and print these pages.

The document is set to print at A4 but you can enlarge pages to A3 by increasing the output percentage using the page set-up settings for your printer.

Throughout the book, you will see this CD icon used:
This indicates that there is electronic material available on the CD-Rom.

CD-Rom Contents

All contents marked P *are full page photocopiable resources*

Chapter 1

Fig 1.1 Children's behaviour and how teachers feel P

Fig 1.2 How Nurture Groups fit with ECM Outcomes P

Fig 1.3 Admission Criteria Checklist P

Chapter 2

Fig 2.1 Process of Strategic Planning

Fig 2.2 Values audit P

Fig 2.3 What is your vision for your nurture group? P

Fig 2.4 Stakeholder analysis P

Fig 2.5 Mission statement criteria P

Fig 2.6 Action plan P

Fig 2.7 Steering Group letter P

Fig 2.8 Weekly Update Sheet P

How to Use this Book

It is relatively easy to set up a nurture group. The school needs a room with some basic equipment, two caring, hard-working adults and a group of children with a variety of emotional and behavioural difficulties. However, there is huge potential for things to go wrong if time is not given for:

- the school to develop an understanding of nurture group principles and practice

- the steering group to plan *how* the nurture group is going to operate

- the school to have opportunities to develop a clear vision for the work of the nurture group.

If a nurture group is set up without this understanding and planning, there can be confusion about what it is supposed to achieve and how it works. There can be uncertainty about which children should be selected and what should they do in the nurture group. School staff can feel dispirited if this is another intervention that does not seem to work.

The objectives of this book are to enable a school to:

- understand the benefit to the whole school of having a nurture group, how the school is able to respond more flexibly to difficult situations and how relationships with particular children can become more positive

- use a proven planning model to successfully manage the development of the nurture group and ensure that it runs successfully

- be clear about which children to select for nurture group placement and have a good understanding of how to work with the children in the nurture group, especially when a child is finding it difficult to manage his behaviour

- organize a daily timetable, work effectively with parents and other professionals and think through how children will be reintegrated to their classes

- understand the importance of supporting the adults working in the nurture group, so that they are not working in isolation.

- develop Behaviour Plans so that the whole school works consistently with particular children

- use INSET materials provided on the CD-Rom to give staff understanding about different aspects of nurture group work, such as using the Boxall Profile, understanding how attachment affects children's behaviour at school and how to use a management model to develop the nurture group.

There are resources from each chapter on the CD-Rom that can be adapted to any setting. INSET material is provided on the CD-Rom in the form of PowerPoint presentations, with accompanying explanatory notes that make the presentations self-contained and very easy to use.

At the end of many of the chapters are suggestions for further reading in the form of books or useful websites.

The aims of this book are:

1   To enable practitioners to plan for the development of a nurture group and successfully manage the changes that will occur within the school

2   To ensure that schools have a clear vision and understanding about the work of nurture groups and how the adults will be working with the children

3   To develop knowledge about how children behave and for this to enable good practice to develop within the school

4   For children, parents, teachers and school staff to be feel the benefit of a well run nurture group and for the whole school community to become a nurturing environment

5   To inspire schools to set up and run the best nurture groups that they can so that the whole school community can work together with empathy and understanding.

1

Why Schools and Children Need Nurture Groups

This chapter covers

> how nurture groups enable schools to meet OFSTED criteria on inclusion
> how nurture groups fit with the Every Child Matters outcomes
> how having a nurture group helps a school adjust to meet the needs of the child, rather than the vulnerable child having to fit in with school demands
> the principles and practice of nurture groups.

Introduction

For children to be successful at school, they need to be able to cope with many requirements. They need to be able to try out and learn new skills, cope with change, face problems, make and keep friends, care about other people, know when things are right and wrong and be able to make positive choices. Children also need to be 'willing to entrust themselves to the teacher' and 'have an awareness of how the world around them functions' and be 'sufficiently organized to attend and follow through what is required' (Boxall, 2002). However, there are children who find it very difficult to cope with what is asked of them at school. For these children, simply being part of a large group, being asked to 'have a go' at a task, or trying to cope with building a relationship with the teacher can be beyond what they can manage. School for these children is a threatening place, which often leaves their feelings and emotions in turmoil. They do not feel safe at school and a great deal of their energy is taken up with managing the anxiety that arises from this feeling. When confronted with demands made by school, these children will attempt to defend themselves from the anxiety, confusion or pain that they are feeling. We all use defences from time to time in our own lives. This is where we put up a psychological barrier that protects us from a perceived threat when interacting with others. When we feel emotionally unsafe we use defences to help us feel safer. For example, we may avoid what is difficult, or deny that there is a problem. We may idealize others and belittle ourselves, or we may rationalize a situation that we are finding difficult.

The defensive process is not in itself a problem. However, problems arise at school when the defence that the child uses gives rise to behaviour that causes difficulties for the child and people around them. This is where a child might display:

- temper tantrums, triggered by the slightest word or action

- aggressive behaviour

- very withdrawn behaviour.

Other children are without the personal resources needed for school. These children have poor personal organization. They have a limited knowledge and understanding about themselves and the world around them. They find it difficult to communicate with adults or children and often appear bewildered. They are restless and easily distracted. They find it hard to think things through and often lack a good attention span. There are also children who become aggressive or have tantrums as well as others who plunge in and grab and who seem unable to regulate their behaviour. There are also children who are very withdrawn at school and who are unable or unwilling to join in with class activities.

These are the children who worry teachers. These are the children who don't seem to 'fit' in the class. Teachers are unsure how to meet the needs of these children. They are anxious about how to build a relationship with the child. Many teachers are unsure of how to manage these children effectively and positively. They are anxious about how the child might react when their behaviour is questioned or confronted. Much of what is tried only seems to work for a limited time, or not to work at all. It often seems that the teachers feel guilty about how they are letting these children down. One teacher who was interviewed by nurture group staff in 2005 described the situation that she found herself in.

> Your whole day really was around this child, from the moment he came in until the moment he left. I felt even though I tried lots of strategies, they would only work in the short term and then they wouldn't work any more. We would implement things such as sticker charts, or giving him a safe place to go … and I just felt that these things worked for maybe one day or two days and then after that, he just wouldn't care about them any more and I felt that these things were quite superficial really.

Schools need to be able to meet the needs of these most vulnerable children. They should have the ability to intervene early when they recognize a child who is unable to cope with the demands of school life. As Marjorie Boxall argues, 'if the child is unable to adjust to the needs of the school, then the school must adjust to meet the needs of the child.' Rather than these children facing anxious or hostile adults at school who are unsure of how to cope with the unpredictable and puzzling behaviour that these children are using to defend themselves from their own anxieties, she suggests that adults in schools ought to respond to children and care for them as if they were their own.

How can schools include these very challenging children? Can nurture groups provide a solution for schools? First we need to see how educationally inclusive practice is defined by OFSTED and the Department of Children, Schools and Families.

Children's behaviour and how teachers feel

(following Ayres et al., 2000)

For many teachers, the behaviour of vulnerable children may present as:

- *incomprehensible* or *inconsequential* or *puzzling*

- *under-achieving* despite proven cognitive ability

- *immature* in comparison to others of the same age

- *phobic*

- *anxious, withdrawn* or *depressed*

- *hostile*

- *unpredictable* in terms of actions and reactions and where no obvious pattern emerges easily.

These children often leave teachers feeling:

- *de-skilled, inadequate* or *helpless* to bring about change or impart skills;

- *angry*

- *despairing*

- *anxious*

- *depressed*

- *isolated.*

OFSTED inclusion criteria

OFSTED says inclusive practice is:

> One in which the teaching and learning, achievements, attitudes and well-being of every young person matter. Effective schools are educationally inclusive schools. This shows ... in their ethos and willingness to offer new opportunities to pupils who may have experienced previous difficulties. This does not mean treating all pupils the same way. Rather it involves taking account of pupils' varied life experiences and needs. (*Evaluating Educational Inclusion: Guidance for inspectors and schools*. OFSTED, 2000:7)

The Department of Children, Schools and Families says:

- the culture, practice, management and deployment of resources in a school or setting are designed to ensure all children's needs are met

- LEAs, schools and settings work together to ensure that any child's special educational needs are identified early

- LEAs, schools and settings exploit best practice when devising interventions. (DfES, 2001)

The question that needs to be asked is how teachers and schools can meet the needs of all children within the mainstream class. How can the school take account of each child's life experiences and hope to create a safe environment within which the child will be able to learn and develop? With the children described above, there has been a breakdown in the care provided by the home or an absence of this care. Whilst at school, these children are in an almost constant defensive state, ready to protect themselves from threat. Their minds often seem to be in turmoil, and because of this turmoil, they are not ready or able to learn. Indeed, their behaviour can mean that it becomes very difficult for the teacher to teach effectively. Heather Geddes, writing in her excellent book *Attachment in the classroom* (Geddes, 2006) argues that:

> Teachers are inadequately prepared for responding to such challenges. There is little training for working with pupils with emotional and behavioural difficulties in initial teacher training ... In this respect, when teachers and other education staff are overwhelmed by the demands of anxious children, the experience of adverse attachment can be replicated. The teacher can become reactive and respond with rejection, criticism and punishment. The pupil can re-experience the overwhelming uncertainties of early infancy which were not adequately contained in the primary Attachment relationship. (Geddes, 2006)

There are two problems facing schools with regard to managing children who demonstrate very difficult behaviour at school.

1   Knowledge and understanding about how children's behaviour is affected by their earliest relationships and experiences is not yet widely available to practitioners in the world of education.

2   Many schools are not sure what to do with children who have emotional and behavioural difficulties. Interventions are put in place once the behaviour has become a problem and this can often be too late both for the child and the school.

Interventions used by schools often originate from the behavioural perspective. This is where children are understood as having learnt inappropriate behaviour, which needs to be unlearned, and more appropriate behaviour learned. From the behavioural perspective, inappropriate behaviour is seen as the result of difficulties that the child is *currently* experiencing. So the emphasis is on attempting to deal with the symptoms rather than the underlying problems. This approach is effective for a range of emotional and behavioural problems and can certainly be used successfully in many cases. However, the behavioural perspective does not address problems where behaviour is understood as being determined by unconscious processes. Interventions coming from this perspective do not take into account underlying causes that may be operating. Instead, the focus is on observable symptoms. The behavioural approach emphasizes changing people's behaviour through external methods.

Because they focus on current patterns of observable behaviour rather than trying to understand what has gone on for the child in their past and how their needs can now be met, these behavioural-based interventions are often not effective in managing the types of behaviours outlined earlier. In this approach there is a focus on what triggers behaviour. Interventions are based on rewarding positive behaviour and setting up situations where the child can be rewarded. The adults involved will make use of positive reinforcement, including stickers or tokens, the use of praise and the child being able to choose preferred activities. Often contracts are used, where an agreement is drawn up between the child and the adults involving behaviours, rewards and sanctions. In practice, these types of intervention seem to work initially, but because the underlying causes of the child's behaviour are not addressed, the same behaviour reappears. Thus the teacher's belief that nothing works for this child is reinforced. For many of these children and the adults who work with them a cycle of failure can develop. The adults are trying to get the child to fit in with what the rest of the children in the class are working on. The child is relying on entrenched patterns of behaviour that get them out of situations that they find impossible to cope with. The child responds negatively to new interventions such as stickers, charts and contracts and the adults feel that they are failing the child again.

Nurture groups are the answer

So it would appear that there is a need for a different approach and this is where nurture groups fit in. Nurture group principles and practice are based on attachment theory. Nurture groups allow schools to intervene proactively to meet children's needs. Nurture groups are about the recognition that something has gone wrong in the early nurturing care of some children and there is now an opportunity to 're-parent'. Nurture groups allow the schools to work flexibly with the children. The children no longer have to fit with the demands of a mainstream class within which they experience stress, anxiety, confusion and failure.

Teachers can feel that they are ill-prepared to meet the demands of children with attachment disorders who are in their classes. There can be a feeling that these children are being let down by the education system and it seems very difficult to understand what these children need and how to work with empathy. This will be looked at more fully later in this chapter. A useful starting point for adults that gives a greater understanding about the needs of the child is *The Boxall Profile Handbook* (Bennathan and Boxall, 1998). This is an assessment tool developed in the early days of nurture group development when it became clear that there needed to be some way of understanding and assessing children's needs. *The Boxall Profile Handbook* enables practitioners to assess children based on their knowledge of how they function around the school. It can be used along with other assessments to build up a more complete picture of how the child is making sense of the world around them, and how the school can begin to respond to meet the child's needs. This will be explained in more detail in Chapter 3 on assessing children.

Every Child Matters outcomes

Nurture groups' philosophy and practice fit extremely well with this legislation. A nurture group enables the school to meet the needs of the difficult-to-reach children. One important aspect of nurture group work is that it is a long-term intervention, and as such an ideal opportunity to build relationships with the family and to work with a range of other professionals to address some of the difficulties the family faces. Figure 1.2 shows how a nurture group can fit in with the Every Child Matters outcomes.

So how does a nurture group work?

A 5-year-old child came to our nurture group having been excluded from another school whilst in the Reception class where he had been described as 'a monster'. He arrived with two thick box folders crammed with reports from a whole range of professionals from educational psychologists to art therapists; paediatricians to health visitors. When the reports were read, they each had a variety of recommendations about how to work with this child. What was missing from all of them was the primary importance of developing a positive relationship with him, through which positive change could be brought about.

After being in the group for a few weeks the mother told us that we were the first people who seemed to like her son.

A nurture group is a specific intervention for particular children. These are children identified as having missed out on early nurturing experiences, because of some form of adversity within the family. These adverse factors might be external to the family or internal and can include:

- bereavement or illness

- moving house

- poverty or deprivation

How nurture groups fit with Every Child Matters outcomes

Be healthy	Stay safe	Enjoy and achieve	Make a positive contribution	Achieve economic well-being
Positive relationships with the adults in the nurture group	Being part of a small group with two adults giving security and stability	School able to meet the needs of the child, rather than the child having to fit in with the demands of the school	Understand need for boundaries and be able to regulate their responses to stressful situations	Early intervention leading to a more positive school career
Routines	Clear behaviour expectations	Children enjoy being part of the nurture groups and attendance improves	Develop positive relationships with adults and children which lessen the development of self-defeating behaviour	Child and family regard school as supportive and positive
Boundaries and 'containment'	Sanctions that are fair and consistent	Appropriate early learning takes place so that the child will be able to reintegrate back to their own class and be more able to reach their potential	Increase a sense of worth and higher self-esteem for the children. Reducing the negative defensive behaviours that becomes an entrenched way of being for the child	Child more able to make better choices due to a more positive Inner Working Model
Cooking with fresh ingredients, going for walks, playing together, chatting, sharing, having fun	Emotional 'containment'			
Sharing daily breakfasts				

- drug or alcohol abuse

- depression

- parents who provide a chaotic or dysfunctional family environment.

For these children, their childhood experiences will have been 'related to developmental impoverishment and loss in the first three years' (Boxall, 2002). What nurture groups are able to do is 'to create the world of early childhood in school and so provide a broadly based learning experience normally gained in the first three years' (Boxall, 2002). To achieve this, nurture group staff would need to:

1   Set up a room in the school with a more homely atmosphere than a normal class and which allows nurture group activities to take place.

2   Develop a structured timetable which allows the staff to be able to provide a slow moving day with its own routines and experiences which are developmentally at the right level for the children in the group, where the children feel secure..

3   Build close attachments with the children, through which much of the work of the nurture group is done.

> A vital aspect of nurture group work is creating the relationship between adult and child so that change can happen.

The first two steps need to be taken in order to create the right environment in which the relationship between the children and the adults can grow. It is this relationship that is essential to the work of the nurture group: through this that the work with the children can take place. However, it is not easy to understand this relationship, or get it right. The fundamental questions that the adults need to address are:

- Who am I when I am in the nurture group?

- How do I need to be for these children?

- How should I respond to the children's needs?

What you would hope to see happening between the adults and the children in a nurture group is 'the attentive, interactive process of mother and toddler in the earliest years' (Boxall, 2002). Through this dynamic, two-way relationship the child will begin to develop an understanding of his own mind. There will be a growing awareness of the complexity of emotional states within himself and other people around him. We would want the children to experience order and pattern in the world and in their own mind and body.

The children need to feel 'contained'

To gain a deeper understanding of this relationship between adult and child in the nurture group it is useful to examine the concept, developed by Wilfred Bion, of the adult as a mental 'container'. The idea is that an adult is able to hold, or contain, the feelings and emotions of the child, and reflect them back in a way that the child can manage.

For this to happen, there needs to be a relationship between the adult and the child where the adult is able to get in contact with the child's mind and through the adult's attention and support, enable the child to grow psychologically. Wilfred Bion suggests that a child's mind begins to develop when they are able to make links between two elements:

- something within themselves: something innate

- something outside themselves: something external.

An example of this is seen in the new-born baby feeding. The sucking reflex which a baby has instinctively is the innate element, but the mother has to be there in the external world for the sucking reflex to be realized. Bion thought that this linking together of the child's readiness for experiences with the corresponding external experience is crucial for the child's mental development. What is vital in this experience is the quality of the linking together. It is not like two magnets sticking together, but is much more intimate, like a baby feeding, or a hand in a glove. This entering of one object into another is known as 'containing'. It is the quality of the linking together which is so important.

R. D. Hinshelwood (1999) outlines three main categories of containing:

1   The container (the adult) reacts to the child by becoming inflexible and refusing to respond to what has arrived in it. The parent is unable to be receptive to the child's needs and feels that they must not give in to the child's demands. There are elements of impatience and wanting to keep the child at arm's length ('I don't know what's the matter with the child'). The parents might feel that the child has a well thought-out campaign against them, and a difficult situation is made worse. Adults using such phrases such as 'I can't take that in' are relevant and meaningful to this emotional experience.

2   The second category is the opposite of the first, in that 'the contained (child or infant) is so powerful that they overwhelm the container, which bursts or in some way loses all its own form and function. A mother's mind can literally go to pieces and she panics or even breaks down' (Hinshelwood, 1999).

3   The third of Bion's categories is what you would hope to see happening between adult and child in the nurture group. Here there is a more flexible relationship, in which the feelings and emotional states of the contained (the child) enter the container (the adult) and have an impact on them. However, the container is able to keep its shape and its function and modify the contained. 'The knack is to feel the dread of the child and still retain a balance of mind. An on-going process of mutual influence and adaptation' (Hinshelwood 1999).

The adult's stability and solidity in the face of the child falling apart seems to be the source of the child developing a level of trust in his surroundings and also in himself. This will over time allow the child to be less reliant on the presence of the nurture group adults, as the process of being contained will have become internalized and they can rely more on their own 'balance of mind'. The relevance of the adult is that there is the possibility now for that child that they can look at what is painful and eventually be able to hold the pain in their own mind.

> To have this understanding of how the relationships should be between the adults and the children in the nurture group is so important. Everything else flows from this.

The child needs to develop an attachment for change to take place

Many children who have lacked the early 'containing' experiences in their family will appear more angry or more withdrawn than other children at school. There is a critical time in early childhood when babies form a bond with their primary caregiver. This bond is called 'attachment'. Babies will behave in ways that bring the primary caregiver to them. They will cry, laugh, reach out, or smile. By responding appropriately to the child, the parent is able to offer comfort and safety. If this happens enough times, the child is able to build a relationship based on reliability, predictability, understanding and trust. The parent has now become a 'secure base' from which the infant can explore the world around itself.

How the child sees itself also develops through this relationship with the parent. Bowlby describes this as the 'internal working model'. If the child develops a secure attachment with the parent, they will see themselves as worthwhile. This will come about through 'the continual and affirming interaction between himself and the attachment figure' (Ayres et al., 2000). However, if the attachment figure is not able to respond in a meaningful way to the child; if they are 'not emotionally available to him significantly or repeatedly' (Ayres et al., 2000) then the child does not develop a positive Inner Working Model. In fact they begin to see themselves as worthless instead of worthwhile. This can lead to the child:

- finding it harder to explore new 'territory', so being asked at school to 'have a go' can be very difficult and threatening

- finding it harder to develop new attachments with teachers and other adults in the school

- being less able to seek help when they find something difficult at school

- feeling threatened when having to share the attention of adults

- being preoccupied with unresolved attachment problems so they are not able to concentrate on learning

- developing behaviours to help cope with the pain and distress they are feeling. These behaviours can often be self-defeating and negative. The longer they are allowed to continue without intervention, the more entrenched they become.

The problems faced by children who have suffered a lack of early nurturing care are profound. Schools can find it very difficult to know what to do in order to take account of what the child has been through and be able to provide opportunities and an environment through which their needs can be met.

Where do you start?

Setting up a nurture group is an effective way for a school to meet their needs, by creating an environment in which it is possible to build the necessary relationship between the adults and the children. It is very important that a nurture group should be well set up so that it can be successful. The following are key considerations.

1   A room (a secure base).

2   The balance must be right between girls and boys, between children who are withdrawn and children with challenging behaviour, and between children of different ages. Is it feasible to put children from the Foundation Stage with children from Key Stage 2?

3   Intervening with children as early as possible in their school life, before behaviours become entrenched.

4   A slow moving day with no surprises, but with plenty of routine and repetition.

5   A more homely atmosphere than a classroom, including soft and cosy places to sit.

6   A small number of children with two adults.

7   Firm boundaries, which are consistent and fair. Firm and clear boundaries are what make 'containing' possible. Boundaries are what make the sides of the container strong enough to be able to contain. Without boundaries, the sides of the container can weaken and the children do not feel contained.

8   Early learning. As Marjorie Boxall says, it is important that these children are seen as though they were one-, two- or three-year-olds or in some cases even younger, and that adults in the nurture group are able to respond to the children at the level of development they are at. The learning will involve providing experiences so that the children can learn about themselves, such as having birthday parties and choosing toys from the local Toy Library. It will also involve developing skills such as turn taking, sharing, developing eye contact and accepting group constraints.

9   Training for the adults involved and for the whole school.

Throughout the setting-up process, and once the group is running, there will be issues and concerns that continue to arise, ranging from how to use *The Boxall Profile Handbook* to how to manage behaviour or build a relationship with a particular child. These and many other concerns will require advice and input from the nurture group staff, and it may well be appropriate to offer regular staff training as a way of developing understanding and expertise within the school community. Nurture group staff will benefit immensely with regard to delivering training 'in house' by developing their own knowledge and confidence from having completed the NGN Certificate courses. These NGN courses are university accredited and cover the theory and practice of nurture groups. They introduce key themes underpinning nurture groups such as theoretical background, organisation, curriculum, monitoring and evaluation.

Selecting children for the nurture group

When we started our nurture group, we knew that it was very important that the selection process was transparent: all staff would need to know which children had been selected and to understand why. To help achieve this transparency, we used:

- knowledge of the child and family background

- an Admission Criteria Checklist

- Goodman's Strengths and Difficulties Questionnaire

- Boxall Profiles.

Transparent communication is so important when considering children for the nurture group. There will need to be a good deal of discussion between relevant staff that will allow the everybody involved to reach the right decision for the child.

The first consideration will be to share knowledge of how the child is managing at school. Staff need to be open and honest about the situation. Teachers can worry that they will be seen as failures if they admit to finding a child difficult, or that they cannot understand or manage a child's behaviour.

Using the Admission Criteria Checklist enables staff to begin to develop a clearer picture of how the child's difficulties have come about. A child should be considered for the nurture group if the majority of the answers are in the 'Yes' or 'To some extent' columns. If the answers are mainly 'No' then other support may be more suitable for that child.

The Goodman's Strengths and Difficulties Questionnaire (www.sdqinfo.com) is a very useful assessment tool to use at this stage. It gives scores that are graded 'normal', 'borderline' or 'abnormal' – 'abnormal' referring not to the child, of course, but to the child's score being different from what might be expected. An 'abnormal' score would be another indicator that the child could benefit from placement in a nurture group. It can be useful for staff to complete this assessment with the parents so that a clearer understanding of their perspective can be achieved.

The Boxall Profile Handbook gives a very clear explanation of such children's difficulties and their origin. Use of this assessment tool will give very clear guidance about nurture group placement.

> The Admission Criteria Checklist indicates the type of behaviours demonstrated by children who have lacked early nurturing care and have attachment issues. The range of behaviours on this checklist show how important it is for nurture group staff to have an understanding of what the children need the adults to be each day. Just caring for the children is not enough. They are bringing their own pain to school each day and the adults have to manage this. Containing the children's emotions and reflecting them back in a way they can manage them is the basis of nurture group work.

Everybody wins!

If a school has a nurture group, there is the potential for the whole school community to benefit immensely.

Understanding

Nurture group principles and practice give schools a much greater insight into children's experiences and how these impact on them at school. The school staff begin to see the world through the eyes of the child and understand what it is that the child needs. The adults can then respond with empathy and understanding.

Hope

Having a nurture group enables the school to respond more positively to challenges presented by some children. Teachers feel relieved that something positive is being offered to the child. Parents are relieved that the school is offering something positive. The child is at last able to relax and begin to enjoy school within an environment where they feel safe and happy.

Flexibility

Having a nurture group means that the school is no longer confined to managing a child in a large class. The nurture group can support the child in a variety of way: support may be full-time or for specific parts of the day, or children can join the group for breakfast or afternoon activities. A balance of support can enable the children to manage the rest of the day in their own class. The school is better able to meet the needs of the child, rather than expecting the child to fit in with the demands of the school, which may be too much for them.

Work with the family

When a child is placed in a nurture group, there is generally a reduction in anxiety for the child and they usually begin to see school more positively. There is good news about

Admission Criteria Checklist

Name............................

Criteria	Yes	To some extent	Don't know	No
Has been through periods of stress sufficiently severe to limit the nurturing process of early years				
Finds it hard to make choices, share, listen, look, remember, know about self				
Finds it hard to manage well in social situations				
Can find it hard to play effectively				
Shows a lack of curiosity about the world around them				
Lacks sympathy				
Often non-compliant				
Lacks self-control				
More angry than other children				
More withdrawn than other children				
More clingy than other children				
Not so able to explore new territory (skills and knowledge)				
Not so able to seek help from adults				
Finds it hard to share attention of adults				
Finds it hard to tolerate frustrations in learning				
Restless, finds it hard to listen				
Behaves aggressively or impulsively				
Withdrawn and unresponsive				
Disturbed by change				
Stressful or anxious				
Over-stimulated by school. Unrestrained behaviour				
Lower self-esteem				
Less positive engagement with others				
Less popular with peers				
Dependent on the adults in the classroom				

the child to communicate to the parents that can lead to the nurture group staff developing positive relationships with the parents. This can begin to lead to the involvement of other professionals who may offer more specific support to the family or the child.

Work with other professionals

Nurture groups work therapeutically with children and this approach allows other professionals to work more effectively and flexibly with the child and the family. The concern now is not about managing difficult behaviour in the class on a day-to-day basis, but is rather more about working on underlying issues affecting the child or the family.

The nurturing school

One of the benefits of having a nurture group is that over time, nurture group practice and principles can impact on whole school practice. This can lead to a change in culture with more emphasis on the importance of developing trusting relationships and developing a child's-eye view of the world.

Key ideas

> There are a number of children who find it very difficult to manage their behaviour at school. They are unable to regulate their responses to situations that they perceive as stressful, and they do not respond to the same reinforcers that motivate a more securely attached child.

> Teachers ask for help, but often the strategies offered only work for a short period of time. Failure of these strategies reinforces the teacher's understanding that they are failing.

> Interventions need to change from being behavioural-based to being based on an understanding of how a child is affected by attachments made with their primary caregiver.

> Nurture groups allow schools to respond flexibly and to meet the needs of more children who find school a difficult place to be.

> Nurture groups need to be set up and run according to principles discussed by Marjorie Boxall and Marion Bennathan.

> Nurture groups fit very well with the Every Child Matters agenda and the understanding that early intervention is vital in supporting children and families.

Further reading

Ayres, H., Clarke, D. and Murray, A. (2000) *Perspectives on Behaviour: A Practical Guide to Effective Interventions for Teachers*. 2nd edn. London: David Fulton.

Bennathan, M. and Boxall, M. (2000) *Effective Intervention in Primary Schools: Nurture Groups*. 2nd edn. London: David Fulton.

Geddes, H. (2006) *Attachment in the Classroom: The Links Between Children's Early Experience, Emotional Well Being and Performance in School*. London: Worth.

2

How to Plan For a Nurture Group in Your Setting

> **This chapter covers**
>
> > the principles behind a Strategic Planning Model; how to use this model to develop a successful nurture group
> > how to set up a Steering Group and what it would expect to achieve
> > how the Strategic Planning Model worked for Kaleidoscope
> > examples of evaluations and how these can feed into the school's Self-evaluation Form.

To develop a nurture group within a school, initial discussions need to take place with the Head Teacher, SENCO and members of the school's senior management team. School governors also need to be involved early on. Discussion should focus on how well the needs of the pupils with emotional and behavioural difficulties are currently being met, and whether these needs could be better met within a nurture group. If there is agreement about the benefits of having a nurture group in school, further discussions need to include the following.

Funding

Each school will have to develop its own funding stream. Money may be available within the school budget, from the Local Education Authority, or it may be worth pursuing other sources, such as the Children's Fund. Advice on funding sources can be found at www.nurturegroups.org.uk.

Staffing

A nurture group run along full Boxall guidelines would have a teacher and an assistant working exclusively in the nurture group. Nurture groups can also be successfully run with two assistants. In both cases, there are always two adults who are involved in the day-to-day running of a nurture group.

A room

The children need a secure base – a room that is theirs. This room will require fitting out with basic equipment, such as tables, chairs, cooker, fridge, play equipment and teaching and learning resources.

Once these initial discussions have taken place, funding has been secured and a suitable room has been found, it is necessary to move on to the planning stage.

How will the group be managed to ensure success over the life of the project? How will people who affect the group, or are affected by it have their values taken into account? How will the success of the group be assessed? How can a Vision and Mission Statement be formulated that will encourage the whole school to view the group with understanding and consistency?

There are five main areas that need to be understood and addressed when developing a nurture group within a school.

1   **The role of the nurture group teacher**   The nurture group teacher has responsibility for planning and organizing learning activities, record keeping, encouraging parental involvement, contact with each child's class teacher, staff development, liaison with outside agencies and the local authority, and working with the assistant in a considerate and co-operative way. The nurture group teacher also needs a voice on the school's senior management team to ensure that nurture group principles and practice are taken on board throughout the school, for example in deciding how the nurture group impacts on the school's behaviour policy.

2   **Whole school integration**   This involves working at developing shared values through disseminating information and understanding to all staff. It will involve organizing regular visits to the nurture group for all staff, and having input to staff meetings. It also requires having measurable objectives that show success.

3   **Selection of children**   The policy on selection criteria needs to be transparent and understood by all.

4   **Involvement of parents**   The majority of contact with parents is likely to be informal, but the importance of regular review meetings needs to be understood, so that parents are kept fully up-to-date with the progress their child is making.

5   **Wider community and other professionals**   This may involve organizing training/INSET with other schools or services such as health visitors and Social Services so that there is an understanding of how a nurture group can support vulnerable children. There is a role here for coordinating provision with other schools, linking with other nurture group practitioners, and accessing support from other professionals such as educational psychologists.

The crucial question that needs to be asked when looking at these areas is 'how?' How can the nurture group teacher ensure that all of the above will be developed successfully? How will the school know if the group is running well and the children making progress? How will the nurture group teacher know if the group is running successfully? How can the school know that the nurture group is having a positive impact on the whole school community?

> Caring is not enough. Changing is not enough. Spending money is not enough. Raising standards is not enough. In fact, each of the single-issue, quick fixes imposed upon education might be failing for the wrong reasons … we have been selecting means (how) before agreeing the ends. It is now time to get ends and means related. Being strategic is knowing what to achieve, being able to justify the direction and then finding the best way to get there. (Kaufman, *Mapping Educational Success: Strategic Thinking and Planning For School*, 1992)

Strategic planning of a nurture group

> Strategic planning provides a technique for establishing and maintaining a sense of direction when the future has become more and more difficult to predict. It is a continuous process by which the organisation is kept on course, through making adjustments as both internal and external factors change … the emphasis is on evolutionary or rolling planning and responding proactively rather than reactively to change. (Weindling, *Understanding School Management*, 1996)

It is useful to see strategic planning as the process by which members of the organization envisage its future and develop the necessary procedures to achieve that future.

Preparation

Every nurture group should have a steering group. The purpose of the steering group is to support, guide, challenge, sustain and champion the work of the nurture group. There needs to be clarity about who should be on the group and how it will operate to ensure nurture group success: a mix of people who can provide insight and experience. The steering group should involve representatives from:

- the school's senior management team

- school staff, such as teachers and classroom assistants

- governors

- teachers/SENCOs from neighbouring schools

- other professionals, such as Social Services

- the Educational Psychology Service

- the local authority.

A good way of starting the process of strategic planning and establishing the steering group is to use one to two whole days to work through the process outlined above.

The Process of Strategic Planning

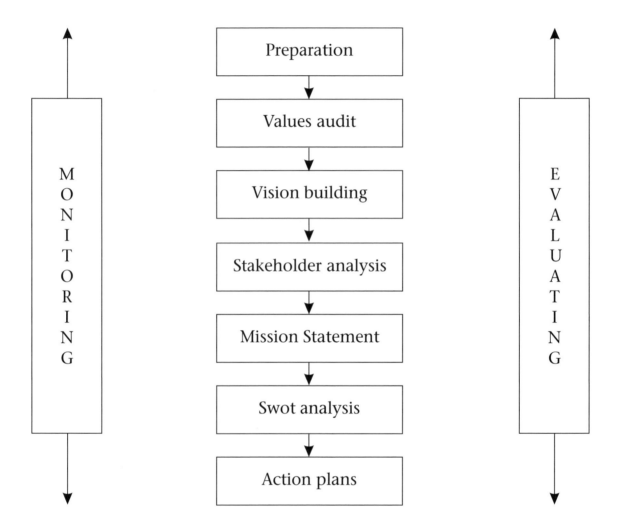

(Adapted from: Dick Weindling, *Understanding School Management*, 1996)

Values audit

This stage involves an analysis of the values of staff and other key stakeholders. When setting up a new project which will have an impact on the whole school it is vital that an opportunity is given for individuals to discuss what they feel and believe about the project. It is important that this happens early in the process so that any differences in values and beliefs can be clarified and, where possible, resolved. It can be argued that any planning that does not take account of values will almost certainly fail. Values audits can be carried out through the use of:

- Questionnaires, where staff could be asked to rate their agreement with a list of values on a five-point scale

- Interviews, where staff could be asked about their beliefs about nurture groups

- A projective technique where staff are asked to write an imaginary diary for a typical day in the future.

The process will reveal a range of opinions. These can include perceiving a nurture group as:

- a place where children would be able to catch up on missed work

- a 'sin-bin'

- a group where the emphasis would be away from any academic activities and much more towards 'nurturing' activities

- a place where 'naughty' children are rewarded with 'nice' activities.

Differences of opinion will probably not be ironed out on one day, but this process will allow a discussion to begin and common ground to be shared. Carrying out a values audit gives a starting point and a structure to the discussion. It also enables the discussion to take on board a wider range of views, beliefs and experiences from the people involved.

Vision building

A clear vision of what the school is hoping to achieve is vital to the success of a new school project such as a nurture group. It cannot be the vision of a single person: a shared vision is necessary to ensure success. There are some important elements to understand about what constitutes an effective vision.

- Visions develop and change over the course of the planning process.

- Visions need to be developed collectively, not solely by one person.

- Visions are important because they give shared meaning. People can talk about the vision, using a common language and know that they are engaged in a common task.

A simple method that can be used to generate the vision is to ask the steering group to imagine what the nurture group would be like in one, two or three years' time. This forms a picture for the group of what could be realistically achieved in the future.

Values Audit

What are your personal beliefs about nurture groups?

What should set a nurture group apart from a mainstream class?

What would you want to see happening in a nurture group?

What would you want to hear children say about nurture groups?

What would you want to hear parents say about nurture groups?

What would you want to hear teachers say about nurture groups?

What would you like to hear other professionals say about nurture groups?

Vision

Think about how you would like the nurture group to be in three years' time – remember to make it achievable. Write down what you would like to see that would be different from now. Think in terms of children, school, parents, other schools, Social Services …

Stakeholder analysis

A 'stakeholder' in a nurture group is someone who can affect it or be affected by it. In this very interesting part of the Strategic Planning Model (Figure 2.1), there is an attempt to analyse the views of the people who have a stake in the nurture group, including teachers, parents, teaching assistants, governors and so on. Carrying out this analysis allows the steering group to understand what these groups expect and require from the nurture group and to what extent the nurture group will meet their concerns. This process allows the steering group to have a better understanding of a wide range of people whose views may not always be taken into consideration. The following table provides a useful format for gathering and analysing this information.

Take the example of teachers. The name of the stakeholder group, teachers, should be entered in the first column. Their importance would be high, as would their involvement. The criteria that they would use to judge the success of the nurture group could be:

- Happier children

- Children more able to manage their behaviour

- Good relationships with parents

- Calmer classrooms.

In the final column a judgement can be made about how well the nurture group meets these criteria. Undertaking this task before the nurture group opens allows the school to have a better understanding of areas that need to be addressed so that the nurture group will run effectively.

> Carrying out a stakeholder analysis simply allows you to put yourself in other people's shoes and to have a more complete picture of the variety of needs that the nurture group will be attempting to meet.

Mission statement

The development of a mission statement is important, as it is the means by which all of the information that has been gathered through the activities outlined above is brought together into a declaration of purpose or intent. The mission statement can be compiled using the six questions in Figure 2.5.

The steering group should use the mission statement as a guide and reference point. It should be used widely to inform people both inside and outside the school about the nurture group.

Stakeholder analysis

Stakeholder groups	Importance: High/med/low	Involvement High/med/low	What criteria do the stake-holders use to assess the performance of the nurture group?	Our judgement of the current performance of the nurture group Poor = 1 Very good = 5

Mission statement

1   Who are we, what is our identity?

2   What are the basic social needs we exist to fill?

3   What do we want to do to recognise and respond to these needs?

4   How should we respond to our key stakeholders?

5   What is our philosophy and what are our core values?

6   What makes us distinctive or unique?

(Weindling, *Understanding School Management*, Unit 6, p. 13)

SWOT analysis

SWOT stands for strengths, weaknesses, opportunities, and threats. The purpose of this activity is to enable the planning group to:

- Build on strengths

- Overcome weaknesses

- Make the most of opportunities

- Minimize threats.

This activity can be carried out by dividing a sheet of paper into quarters with each quarter being labelled Strengths, Weaknesses, Opportunities and Threats. Then the group 'brainstorms' a list of strengths and weaknesses within the school that could have an impact on the nurture group. The steering group should then list external trends that could affect the development of the nurture group over the next three years. These trends might be seen as opportunities or threats. It would also be worthwhile considering each of the threats or opportunities and how likely they are to occur, as well as whether they will have a significant impact on the new project. It is then possible to focus on the trends that are likely to have the most impact on the nurture group.

Action plans

The final stage in the strategic planning process is to draw up action plans. This is to specify:

- tasks that need to be carried out

- people to complete the tasks

- dates by which tasks need to be completed

- criteria by which to identify success.

These action plans can be completed on a simple table, such as the one below. Figure 2.6 is a blank table on the CD-Rom. These are examples of actions that may come up during this planning process. However, they will be different for each school.

Action	Who?	When?	Success criteria
Children selected for nurture group using agreed Admission Process	Nurture group staff, Class teacher, Head teacher, SENCO	Autumn Term	Children selected. Parental agreement. Transparent selection process
Equipment ordered for room. Budget agreed	Nurture group staff, School Secretary	Autumn Term	Room equipped for use
Staff Meeting on 'What is a nurture group?'	Nurture group staff	Autumn Term	INSET carried out leading to increased understanding of nurture principles

Why bother with strategic planning?

Schools continually have to cope with change. Many of these changes are far-reaching and often the consequences of these changes are unclear. There have been changes to the structure of the service, ranging from how the curriculum is taught to how schools are inspected, as well as changes in school culture and expectations about how a school should serve the community. An important management responsibility is to help colleagues to understand and cope with changes created in their work.

The Strategic Planning Model gives a structure to the kind of discussions that the steering group need to have so as to make a clear vision for the nurture group. Although it may be easier to start a nurture group without this preparation, it would be short-sighted and inevitably lead to problems within the school. Having a nurture group will bring about challenges and changes for the school, including how adults relate to children, how behaviour is understood and managed, how children's achievement is measured, how teachers work with parents and how other professionals are involved. These and other issues must be thought about and discussed so as to develop an agreed vision; otherwise, the nurture group may not function successfully within the school. Clarity of vision is required, with the whole school understanding the role of the nurture group; without this, the work of the group will be compromised and the benefit to the children, parents and teachers minimized.

How does it work in practice?

Kaleidoscope's Steering Group

When the funding was in place for our nurture group and I was appointed as the nurture group teacher, I wrote to a selection of colleagues asking if they would like to join Kaleidoscope's steering group. These included:

- the head teacher and deputy head from the school
- the head teacher from a neighbouring middle school
- a deputy head from a neighbouring first school
- a representative from Social Services
- a representative from NCH
- the school's educational psychologist
- a representative from the local authority
- a school parent governor.

This letter forms Figure 2.7.

All of the above agreed to be part of the steering group and we met together for one initial day's planning using the Strategic Planning Model as outlined above. This was a very successful day, which resulted in a clear vision for the nurture group and a Mission Statement, which we were able to share with all school staff. Each year we review these to update them and also to hold them in front of us to ensure that we are staying true to agreed principles.

Completed examples of the Vision, Values Audit and Mission Statement from Kaleidoscope can be found in Appendix 1 and the CD-Rom.

The Weekly Update Sheet

The Weekly Update Sheet is a useful tool that enables nurture group staff to think ahead and be aware of any situations or problems that will impact on the success of the nurture group. It helps the school develop contingency plans so that the school can respond proactively rather than reactively to situations that could impact on the nurture group. This form can be shared every week with the head teacher and relevant members of the school's senior management team to ensure that communication is as good as it can be.

Evaluating the nurture group

Once the strategic planning process has been worked through, the school is in a much better position to judge the effectiveness of the nurture group. There should be agreement about its principles and practice. Meaningful evaluations can then be carried out, to be shared with the steering group; data can also be included in the school's Self-Evaluation Form.

We have evaluated the work of Kaleidoscope each year and it has become possible to follow the progress of nurture group children once they have been back in their classes for a period of time. This kind of follow-up enables the school to support the children more effectively in their classes.

The evaluations comprise:

• Parental questionnaires

• Staff questionnaires

• Interviews with parents and other professionals

• Interviews with children

• Goodman's Strengths and Difficulties Questionnaire (which can be downloaded from www.sdqinfo.com).

Weekly update sheet

Key risks (An event that may occur in the future which will have an adverse effect on the project)	Potential impact	Probability	Contingency

Key issues (A problem that is impeding the progress of the project about which no agreement has been reached)	Priority	Action plans

Tasks completed this week

Tasks to complete next week

Goodman's Strengths and Difficulties Questionnaire (SDQ)

> There are many versions of the SDQ as well as translations in over 60 languages. In a multicultural society, it is very important that the people running nurture groups are familiar with the website so that they feel comfortable downloading appropriate versions that allow parents to respond in their mother tongue. Scoring is still straightforward since the order of items and the scoring rules are identical in every language. What I have found in the past is that if people are presented with a version of the SDQ in the back of a book, they use this even when it is not appropriate – hence the push to get them to know the websites (which also gives them access to scoring instructions, scoring programmes, norms and abstracts from relevant scientific papers). (Goodman, 2007)

The Goodman's Strengths and Difficulties Questionnaires contain 25 criteria against which the children are assessed. The assessments are based on observations of how the child copes with school life. The 25 criteria comprise five scales with five criteria in each scale. Completion of this assessment gives a score for each scale as well as a total score. The scores are classified as normal, borderline or abnormal. These terms refer to the scores, not the children. For our evaluations, we recorded the scores of eighteen children on two dates in a table like the one below, using letters to code for individual children.

SDQ scores

	SDQ 1 Sept 2001	SDQ 2 May 2002
Normal		a, b, c, e, g, h, j, m, n
Borderline	a, b, e, f, n	d, f
Abnormal	c, d, k, l, g, h, j, m	k, l

The first SDQ was completed whilst the children were in their mainstream classes and the second one in the nurture group.

Useful and interesting evaluations can be carried out using these methods. Staff use them to reflect on practice and develop a clear idea of whether the nurture group is effective. Over time it is possible to track how well children are managing in their own classes. By analysing the SDQ from year to year, we were able to see that many children go back to class less worried and anxious and with fewer behaviour difficulties or peer problems. However, there often appears to be continuing issues with:

- restlessness

- fidgeting

- being easily distracted

- finding it hard to think things out before acting

- seeing tasks through to the end.

Questionnaire for parents

	Agree 0	1	2	3	4	Disagree 5
I feel my child has benefited from their time in the Nurture Group						
I have been given enough information about the Nurture Group						
I have been kept up to date with my child's progress						
I have found Nurture Group staff approachable and helpful						
I feel that the Nurture Group has had a positive effect on my child at home						
I feel that the Nurture group has had a positive effect on my child at school						
I think my child gets on better in their own class now						
I think the Nurture Group has a positive effect on the whole school						

Additional Comments

Questionnaire for school staff

	Disagree				Agree
I think the Nurture Group has had a positive effect on the children at this School.					
I think the Nurture Group has had a positive effect on the adults at this School.					
Having a child from my class in the Nurture Group has benefited the other children in my class.					
Having a child from my class in the Nurture Group has been a positive experience for me.					
I have been able to discuss with Nurture Group staff any problems that have arisen with the children.					
I would have liked more opportunities to discuss issues and problems with Nurture Group staff.					
I would like opportunities to visit the Nurture Group.					
I feel that I have a good understanding of what a Nurture Group is and how children are helped.					
I feel that the children who have attended the Nurture Group have made good progress in functioning at school.					
I feel that the children who have attended the Nurture Group have made good academic progress.					
I think that the Nurture Group helps to prevent children failing at school.					
I feel that my professional skills have been developed through understanding about Nurture Groups.					
I get support with children who I find difficult.					

Any other comments

Once we had identified these difficulties, staff were able to work on these skills with particular children using an approach based on the work of Donald Meichenbaum. In his book *Cognitive Behaviour Modification* (1975), he talks about the importance of 'inner speech'. This is where we talk to ourselves when we are solving a problem, or developing a plan of action. Inner speech is most evident when we are attempting a new skill such as learning to drive a car and we might actually talk to ourselves out loud, 'Don't forget, mirror, signal, manoeuvre.' As we get more confident with this new skill, the need to use inner speech diminishes. Meichenbaum categorizes children as either cognitively impulsive or cognitively reflective and his research has shown that in impulsive children there is less use of inner speech. Meichenbaum argues that it is possible to teach such children:

1   to be clear about what they are being asked to do

2   to develop strategies to enable them to carry out the task

3   to use the strategies they have developed so that they experience success.

The adults model the use of 'inner speech' and appropriate behaviour and the children are helped to develop personal 'plans' for different situations within the classroom.

The importance of planning

Is it really worth bothering using a Strategic Planning Model to set up a nurture group?

On one level it is relatively easy to set up a nurture group. The school provides a room and two adults who can set up a timetable based around plenty of routine and structure for the children. There will be opportunities for play as well as appropriate academic activities. Children who are difficult to manage in class will benefit from being in a smaller group and they will be easier to manage. A school can continue to operate as it always has; with the work of the nurture group just being one of many interventions carried on each day.

Or a nurture group can transform a school.

The principles upon which nurture group work is based challenge established and accepted practices and beliefs that currently abound in the education system. Having a nurture group empowers teachers and allows them to respond to children and their problems in a far more positive and empathic way. An effective and well-run nurture group will bring about change within the school culture, ethos and practice. Relationships will change. Beliefs and practice will be challenged. Change can happen.

All of this needs to be managed. Without effective management, problems and difficulties will occur which will have to be responded to reactively.

Use of the Strategic Planning Model allows the school to articulate the challenges of having a nurture group. It allows the school to see where it would like to be and to put appropriate actions in place to achieve its aims. It enables the school community to develop a shared vision and a clear view of what the nurture group can achieve. It ensures that the nurture group staff have a voice within the management structure of the school. It is vitally important that staff working therapeutically within the school know that they are managed and supported.

What happens next?

This can all appear rather daunting, especially in the world of education, where teachers are not used to thinking about 'management'. Many of the terms used seem unfamiliar and rather 'corporate'. It is important to remember that this model is simply a structure that allows focused discussions to take place before decisions are made, so that the decisions made are more likely to be along the right lines.

Once the model has been worked through, the school will have a much better understanding of what resources will be required for the nurture group to function successfully.

Once the 'management' discussions have taken place, various practical decisions will need to be taken. Some of the key considerations are discussed below.

Where will you put the nurture group?

A room which is a safe base is vital. The nurture group needs its own room, which is a sanctuary for the children.

What will be in this room?

It is useful to think of this room as a cross between a homely environment and a classroom. Many resources that would be found in a nursery would be appropriate in a nurture group. Ideally there will be a kitchen area with cooker, fridge, cupboards and worktops. There will be cooking equipment as well as plates, cups and cutlery. There will need to be tables and chairs for eating and working. A mirror is very important. A Home corner, sand and water play, plenty of shelves for toys, games, puzzles, and general equipment. A computer with interactive whiteboard is a fantastic resource, as is a CD player and DVD player with a television. There needs to be soft seating and cushions, and a bookcase with books. If possible a second smaller room within this room, or a partitioned section should be available for children to go when they need or want to be quiet or alone. Easy access to a toilet area is very useful as well.

Food

Cooking together and eating together are a big part of a nurture group. These activities require some form of finance, through either the school budget or voluntary donations from parents. This will be up to the school to decide, but it does need consideration as costs can mount up.

Special resources

Going out for walks in the local area, to the shops or the park or just down to the local river all play a part in the nurture group week. High visibility jackets are very useful for safety and a selection of spare coats, wellington boots and waterproofs are all desirable.

Who should I involve?

You will have the support and input of the head teacher and the senior management team, who will have had input on the steering group. Many school staff and other professionals will also be very interested to see what is going on with the development of the new nurture group. There needs to be a balance between getting up and running and inviting people in to visit. It can be a good idea to have Open Days or Weeks so that you remain in control and the children can be prepared for visitors.

When should I open?

There is a great deal of preparation and organization that needs to happen before a new nurture group can open. It is important not to be rushed into opening before the room is ready or the resources are in place, otherwise the disturbances to the children will be too much for them to cope with. The school should always be thinking about meeting the needs of the children and ensuring that they feel safe and secure.

Key ideas

> There are five main areas that require consideration when planning to open a nurture group. These include the role of the staff, whole school integration, selection of pupils, working with parents and working with other professionals. These are all important and interlinked; all require thought and planning before a nurture group opens to ensure that the group can operate with success.

> The Strategic Planning Model outlined in this chapter gives a framework for discussions to take place so that an agreed way forward can be arrived at.

> The Strategic Planning Model allows the nurture group staff to evaluate the effectiveness of the group and this can feed into the school's Self-Evaluation Form. It is really important that nurture groups evaluate the work they do so that everyone is aware of success stories. Through evaluation and feedback to the steering group, the nurture group staff are much more able to ensure that the group is staying true to nurture group principles and practice.

> Once the strategic management discussions have taken place and there is broad agreement about the role and purpose of the nurture group, there need to be discussions about the room, the resources, a budget and when the nurture group will open.

Further reading

Bennett, N., Crawford, M. and Riches, C. (eds) (1992) *Managing Change in Education. Individual and Organizational Perspectives*. London: Paul Chapman.

Preedy, M. (ed.) (1993) *Managing the Effective School*. London: Paul Chapman.

3

Assessing Which Children Belong in a Nurture Group and Working with Them

---

This chapter covers

> what we should look for when assessing children
> using and interpreting the Boxall Profile
> how the Boxall Profile is used in Kaleidoscope
> using Goodman's SDQ
> effective approaches to working with children with emotional and behavioural difficulties
> how the brain is affected by trauma and the implications for nurture group work
> understanding the level at which the children are functioning and how to meet their needs.

What we should look for when assessing children

Nurture group intervention is for children with a particular set of needs which cannot be met in the mainstream class. Their difficulties are profoundly linked to 'circumstances of stress and adversity sufficiently severe to limit or disturb the nurturing process of the earliest years' (Boxall, 2002). These children find it difficult to:

• trust adults and make relationships

• share attention of adults and other children

• ask for help

- explore the world around them

- tolerate frustrations

- know about themselves

- regulate their responses to stress and anxiety

- have a feeling of self-worth.

Children who are suffering from 'the effects of deprivation of primary care' (Ayres et al., 2000) can also be 'preoccupied with unresolved attachment problems' which makes learning all but impossible.

It is important that we identify such children so that we make the right choices for nurture group placement. The key elements (Ayres et al., 2000) that need to be identified through assessment are:

- for these children, aspects of the learning situation trigger unconscious processes

- pupils are still meshed in emotional conflict generated by earlier experiences

- their behaviour has a meaning of which the pupil is not consciously aware but which directs/influences perceptions of self, others and the learning task.

Furthermore, Marjorie Boxall (2002) identifies two groups of children for whom nurture group provision will be appropriate.

Nurture children

These are children who are functioning below the age of three and have 'considerable emotional, behavioural and learning difficulties' (Boxall, 2002). These difficulties can include being 'preoccupied with an excluding, often bizarre routine' and being fixed 'on a single aspect of experience'. There can also be poor language development (Boxall, 2002). Nurture children can also demonstrate unrestrained behaviour, where they 'plunge in and create havoc'. The families of these children will be identified as being chaotic and disorganized, where there is a lack of routines and boundaries, or alternatively, the limits set will have been 'rigid and uncompromising'. Marjorie Boxall argues that all of the difficulties that the child displays at school that indicate that they are right for nurture group placement are 'related to developmental impoverishment and loss in the first three years' (2002).

Children who need nurturing

Marjorie Boxall (2002) describes these children as those who are 'emotionally disorganised, but were not without the basic learning of the earliest years'. They are able to manage themselves to some degree, but they are children who are 'disturbed and disorganised by stress and anxiety'. She goes on to argue that the structure of the nurture group day and the reassuring relationships offered by the staff lead to children who become more able to manage the demands of school.

A model for carrying out effective assessments

Harry Ayres et al. (2000) suggest a five-stage model for planning interventions:

1   Understand *why* a particular child has been identified.

2   Be clear about *what* the child's main problem is.

3   Think *why* the child has this problem.

4   Agree *what* will be the most effective intervention for this child.

5   *Evaluate* the effectiveness of the intervention.

This can be a very useful model to use when considering which children should be placed in the nurture group.

Using and interpreting the Boxall Profile

The key assessment tool for nurture groups is the Boxall Profile. It provides 'a framework for the structured observation of children in the classroom … Its purpose was to provide a means of assessing the areas of difficulty of severely disadvantaged and deprived children, so as to enable teachers to plan focused intervention'. (Bennathan and Boxall, 1998). It is found within *The Boxall Profile Handbook* and it is essential that the assessment be used with the handbook, as this shows how to interpret the findings. The handbook also contains much useful information on how to use the profile forms.

The profile itself is in two sections:

1   developmental strands, consisting of 'items which describe different aspects of the developmental process of the pre-school years' (Boxall, 1998)

2   the Diagnostic Profile, consisting of items 'describing behaviours that inhibit or interfere with the child's satisfactory involvement in school. They are directly or indirectly the outcome of impaired learning in the earliest years' (Boxall 1998).

In the first section, the developmental strands are arranged in two clusters:

•   organization of experience

•   internalization of controls.

The first cluster is made up of aspects of a child's development which 'describe a child who is organised, attentive and interested, and is involved purposefully and constructively in events, people and ideas' (Boxall, 1998). The second cluster describes a child who is 'emotionally secure, makes constructive and adaptive relationships, is able to co-operate with others, and had internalised the controls necessary for social functioning'.

The second section, the Diagnostic Profile, has three clusters:

- self-limiting features

- undeveloped behaviour

- unsupported development.

The first cluster reflects 'different levels of awareness and functioning, but have in common the lack of a normal thrust for growth' (Boxall, 1998). Children with high scores on the second cluster have had 'too little help in the early years to provide them with the inner resources to relate to each other and engage at an age-appropriate level'. The handbook suggests that these children will benefit from being in a nurture group where appropriate experiences and relationships can be provided for them. High scores in the third cluster 'suggest that the child has suffered a profound lack of early nurturing care, probably associated with intrusively negative experience' (Boxall, 1998). It is likely that these children will develop negative behaviours as a defence against the pain and hurt that they experience. The handbook also suggests that this behaviour becomes entrenched the longer that it is allowed to go on and it then becomes very difficult to change.

As it is an assessment tool based on observations, the Boxall Profile should only be used once the adults have got to know the children. 'Confronted with a child whose anxiety provoking behaviour seems to make no sense, the Profile is where you start. It gives insights and suggests points of entry into the child's world' (*The Boxall Profile Handbook,* 2007) It is also important to understand that the handbook doesn't give specific answers to a child's problems, but allows you to begin to see the world through the child's eyes and to begin to understand the child. It enables you to ask the question, 'Why do I think this child behaved in this way and what does that mean for the approach I use?' (Visser, 2002). The understanding about the child that the Profile gives 'provides the basis upon which the pupil can begin to feel valued and understood (and) it provides an understanding as to why the EBD [emotional and behavioural difficulties] has occurred' (Visser, 2002). The causes of emotional and behavioural difficulties are often complicated and systemic, involving home and school. Without empathy and understanding, the practice of some adults within schools can exacerbate children's difficulties.

When to use the Boxall Profile

Early intervention is an important aspect of nurture group work. If teachers, classroom assistants, or other professionals such as health visitors have concerns about a particular child, then it will be worthwhile using the Boxall Profile so that the adults involved can gain a foundation for their understanding of the child.

The Boxall Profile can correct the adult's misconceptions of a child, highlighting a wider range of concerns that might not be initially obvious. It can be used to inform other professionals. Because it helps to give an understanding of behaviours, it enables the adults working with a child to build a relationship with them and have insight on which to work with the child.

Using the Profile can also help in discussion with parents. Transparency in communication is very important, and talking through what the Boxall Profile shows helps ensure that the school and the parents are seeing the child from the same viewpoint and can work together more effectively.

If the Boxall Profile is used regularly, then it can help with tracking a child's progress.

What the Boxall Profile might reveal about a child

- Insecure, fragile self-image

- Self-defeating behaviour

- Entrenched behaviour, bringing power and satisfaction

- Slow to trust, needing a very tentative approach

- Very insecure

- Seeking attachment, but lacking trust in adults' intentions

- Change is a long and arduous process, both for the child and the adult

- Chaotic home life/inconsistent care or support/too high expectations coupled with too little support to meet them

- Severe lack of self-worth

- At an early stage of development

- Impulse-driven, does not reflect on, monitor or direct own behaviour.

Not all of these features will be present in every child, but these are the features that come up most often and reflect a typical nurture group child.

How the Boxall Profile is used in Kaleidoscope

The Boxall Profile Handbook enables practitioners to interpret the assessment scores and compile a report. The examples below are typical of the reports that can be compiled using the Boxall Profile and the handbook. They give real insight and help the adults to better understand how the child sees the world and their place in that world. It can be seen the child is facing many difficulties on a daily basis, and that much of what has gone on in their lives continues to have a profound effect on them. The challenge for the adults in the nurture group is to be able to create the appropriate environment, experiences and relationships to give the child a better understanding of who they are, so they can recognize feelings and emotions which they are more able to manage.

REPORT 1

Section 1

(Name) can find it hard to heed the teacher and give attention. She finds it very hard to function and conform in a group, have regard for others and accept organizational constraints and requirements. She is not able to express her own needs or accept and accommodate those of others. (Name) finds it hard to identify with others and respect their needs. She lacks self-control and internalized constraints. (Name) is not yet emotionally secure. She finds it hard to make constructive and adaptive relationships where she co-operates with others. She has not yet internalized the controls necessary for social functioning.

Section 2

(Name) will need much individual attention to establish a relationship before she can be drawn into the group. (Name) is impulse driven and does not reflect on, monitor or direct her own behaviour. Personal organization and identity are undeveloped. This would suggest that (Name) has not been helped to gain the resources needed to relate to others and engage at an age-appropriate level. However, there is available potential for attachment and growth if the appropriate relationships and experiences are provided. She tends to seek attachments indiscriminately. (Name) needs a close and consistently supportive relationship. There is deep insecurity about personal worth and adult regard and (Name) finds it hard to trust others. She demonstrates the greedy, grabbing behaviour of the young and undeveloped child.

(Name) is oversensitive to real or imagined slights or threats. This shows itself in defensive and resentful behaviour or in anger directed at others. She has developed a well-organized way of being that increasingly brings satisfaction and power. Behaviour which began as a defence has become an entrenched pattern the longer that it has been allowed to persist. Giving up these immediate and powerful benefits will be a long and arduous process both for the child and the adults.

(*The Boxall Profile Handbook*, 2007)

REPORT 2

(Name) has an insecure, fragile self-image and self-defeating behaviour. (Name) is very sensitive about his worth because of inconsistent care and support and chaotic experience. (Name) has a need for warm attachment, but a severe lack of self-worth makes it difficult for him to seek this.

(Name) has had too little help in the early years to provide him with the inner resources to relate to and engage at an age-appropriate level. (Name) has a marked need for an early level relationship as he is still at an early stage of development. He is impulse driven and does not reflect on, monitor or direct his own behaviours. He has had too little help in the early years, but there is potential for attachment and growth if appropriate relationships and experiences are provided. There is deep insecurity about personal worth and adult regard and (Name) needs a close and consistently supportive relationship.

(Name) has a real lack of trust in others and a tentative approach is needed. It may be some time before trust is established. (Name) has internalized profound insecurity. He feels unvalued and is nursing the pain of a severely injured sense of self. This is expressed in silent negativism, and is projected onto others who are seen as persecutors. This suggests that (Name) fears the adult's reaction to an overt expression of anger, probably because he has not been 'held' when younger in a trusting and supportive relationship.

(*The Boxall Profile Handbook*, 2007)

How to use these reports effectively

The Boxall Profile Handbook gives insight and understanding and allows us to work more empathically with the children, but it does not tell us what we should do or how we should be so that we can meet the needs of the children. Dan Hughes has produced two lists of guidelines that can help nurture group staff. Used in conjunction with *The Boxall Profile Handbook*, it provides the adults with recommendations that can help them be clearer about how to work with the children. The guidelines are:

1   To promote the capacity for fun and love

2   To facilitate effective discipline.

The two sets of principles were written for parents or a child's primary caregivers to enable 'dyadic, integrative parenting with traumatised, attachment-resistant children'. Much of what is included in these principles is appropriate for nurture group practice and can help the adults to understand how they should be with the children when they are in the nurture group. The principles outlined by Dan Hughes help adults to create and maintain a nurture group environment where the children can experience fun, love, safety and containment and be able to flourish, maybe for the first time in their lives.

TO PROMOTE THE CAPACITY FOR FUN AND LOVE

> Affective attunement (the process of getting in tune with the feelings and emotions of another)

> Stay physically close

> Eye contact, smiles, touch, hugs, rocking, movement, food

> Emotional availability in times of stress

> Surprises

> Holding your child

> Make choices for him and structure his activities

> Reciprocal communication of thoughts and feelings, shared activities

> Humour and gentle teasing

> Basic safety and security

> Opportunities to imitate parents

> Spontaneous discussions of past and future

> Routines and rituals to develop a mutual history

TO FACILITATE EFFECTIVE DISCIPLINE

> Stay physically close

> Make choices for him and structure his activities

> Set and maintain your favoured emotional tone, not your child's

> Accept thoughts, feelings and behaviours of child

> Provide natural and logical consequences for behaviours

> Be predictable in your attitude, less predictable in your consequences

> Reattunement following shame-inducing experiences

> Use paradoxical responses

> Use permission, thinking, practising, having limits, being supervised

> Employ quick, appropriate anger, not habitual anger or annoyance

> Reciprocal communication of thoughts and feelings

> Be directive and firm, but also attuned to the affect of your child

> Greatly limit your child's ability to hurt you, either physically or emotionally

> Integrate and resolve own issues from own attachment

(Hughes, 2000)

Using Dan Hughes's principles and guidelines with *The Boxall Profile Handbook*, it is possible to respond effectively to the child's needs that have been highlighted by the Boxall Profile. These recommendations can be useful for Individual Education Plans (IEPs) and discussions with school staff so that the adults at school can better understand the child's needs and respond with consistency.

REPORT 1

Recommendations:

- For the adults to stay physically close to (Name), make choices for him and structure his activities

- To provide natural and logical consequences for behaviours

- The development of routines and rituals to develop a mutual history

- Using permission, thinking, practising, and having limits, being supervised.

REPORT 2

Recommendations:

- For the adults to stay physically close, with plenty of eye contact, smiles, touch, hugs, rocking, movement, food

- Adults to be emotionally available at times of stress

- Holding

- Routines and rituals to develop a mutual history

- Provide natural and logical consequences for behaviours

- Be predictable in attitude.

When we are faced with children who have profound needs, which we can find difficult to make sense of, being able to refer to principles such as those outlined above can be very supportive and enable us to provide the boundaried, containing relationships needed by the children.

Using Goodman's Strengths and Difficulties Questionnaire

This is an invaluable assessment tool to use in the nurture group setting (www.sdqinfo.com). It complements the Boxall Profile extremely well and there is much to be gained from using both assessments. Within the SDQ there are 25 descriptive phrases such as 'Considerate of other people's feelings', 'Rather solitary, tends to play alone' and 'Many worries, often seems worried' (Goodman, 1999).

The adults assess the child on the basis of their behaviour over the previous six months. The following categories are scored as either normal, borderline or abnormal, and a Total Difficulties score can be given as well:

- emotional symptoms

- conduct problems

- hyperactivity

- peer problems

- prosocial behaviour.

There are major benefits of using the SDQ with the parents. It helps to focus on different aspects of the child and so gives starting points for discussion. It gives insight into the child's world. Behaviour which initially appears difficult can be seen from a different perspective and more easily understood.

> If the SDQs are used regularly, the scores can be used to monitor progress as well as to pinpoint the areas where the child is having difficulties so these can be addressed.

Effective approaches to working with children with emotional and behavioural difficulties

The eternal verities

The world of education is in a state of continual change. There are seemingly endless new initiatives and approaches for every aspect of school life, from curriculum to managing behaviour. Constant change can lead to uncertainty and lack of confidence about what works, especially when it comes to meeting the needs of children with emotional and behavioural difficulties. Within a nurture group setting the work of the adults is to build positive and affirming relationships with the children. The adults need to feel confident in how they are working with the children, and that they are relying on principles that have stood that test of time. John Visser (2002) refers to these approaches or principles as 'eternal verities'. These truths are the 'core factors which must be present if any intervention is to meet successfully the needs of children and young people with EBD' (Visser, 2002). They are the set of beliefs, values or ideas that underpin all successful approaches regardless of the setting and 'they carry values and beliefs about the human condition and the quality of life to which we, and especially pupils with EBD are entitled' (Visser, 2002). They are essential because they enable practitioners to have a benchmark from which to reflect on their practice and they also help the practitioners to persevere when the work becomes difficult.

Eternal Verities: a possible list

1   Behaviour can change: emotional needs can be met

2   Intervention is second to prevention

3   Instructional reactions

4   Transparency in communications

5   Empathy and equity

6   Boundaries and challenge

7   Building positive relationships

8   Humour.

Behaviour can change: emotional needs can be met

Many of the children who come to the nurture group are unable to function successfully in the mainstream class. They may be more angry than other children or more withdrawn. They may find it hard to trust the adults in the class or they may find it hard to share the attention of the adult with other children. They may have difficulties attempting new tasks and they might not be able to regulate their emotional responses to stressful situations that occur in the class. They may be insecure. They may have developed ways of behaving that defend them from the pain and turmoil that they feel, but they are self-defeating and negative. These are the children whose behaviour is viewed as incomprehensible to the adults at school. Nurture group staff must view behaviour as capable of being changed. This eternal verity views children as being able to change and understands 'that to be human is not to be at the mercy of instincts or genetic make-up' (Visser, 2002). This belief in the child's ability to change enables the adults working with these children to hold them in high esteem and be prepared to put in the extra effort required to ensure success.

Intervention is second to prevention

Early identification and prevention are key principles that underpin the work of nurture groups. The work is with children who find it hard to function at school, where these difficulties are linked with the child's early relationships and attachments. The Boxall Profile allows the school to recognize where there are gaps in the child's early development as well as the types of behaviour that indicate that a child is finding school difficult. Having a nurture group allows a school to work in a preventative way with children rather than having to use intervention strategies later on to manage failing situations. Children can develop patterns of behaviour that have the purpose of defending them from the pain that they are feeling at school. Over time, these behaviours become more and more entrenched and it becomes increasingly difficult to manage the child and for them to function successfully at school. Children with difficulties linked to their early relationships need to be identified as early as possible by the school so that the nurture group is able to work proactively rather than reactively.

Instructional reactions

For many of the children in the nurture group, there is a lack of awareness about how they behave and the reactions that their behaviours cause. There are aspects of school that trigger feelings of fear and anxiety for the child. Often, these feelings arise from 'unresolved emotional difficulties caused by unconscious conflicts or pre-occupations' (Ayres et al., 2000). The children are still caught up in 'emotional conflict generated by earlier experiences' (Ayres et al., 2000). Much of the behaviour stems from children's need to protect and defend themselves. This 'eternal verity' recognizes the importance of working with the child to help them to understand 'the relationship between cause and effect and how they can achieve different reactions which meet their needs (Visser, 2002). Often the child's behaviour can be self-defeating. They respond in inappropriate ways to the anxiety that they are experiencing. An important aspect of the adult's role in the nurture group is to help the children manage their response to the anxiety that they feel at school. There needs to be time given to explore why the child's reactions are inappropriate, together with exploration of alternatives, so that the child can develop behaviour that is not self-defeating.

Transparency in communications

Transparent communication is central to an effective nurture group. There will be communication between adults at school as well as between school and parents. This communication will be both formal and informal. Systems will need to be set up to ensure that communication is 'clear, consistent and coherent' (Visser, 2002). Transparent communication enables all the adults involved to talk about the child from a shared viewpoint and helps them work towards the same ends. Use of questionnaires with teachers and parents is a useful method. Use of assessments such as the Boxall Profile and the Goodman's SDQ is also essential in developing good communication.

Empathy and equity

John Visser (2002) defines empathy as 'that ability to begin to see the world through the eyes of the child's experience'. He argues that empathy enables the practitioners to continuously ask 'why do I think this child behaves in this way and what does that mean for the approach I use?' Most importantly, empathy 'provides the basis upon which the pupil can begin to feel valued and understood. Being empathetic should not lead to excusing the EBD, rather it provides and understanding as to why the EBD has occurred' (Visser, 2002). Empathy and understanding can lead to approaches that are more likely to work. Again the use of *The Boxall Profile Handbook* and the Goodman's SDQ are essential in helping empathy develop.

Boundaries and challenge

Pupils who have emotional and behavioural difficulties need the school to reduce the number and severity of situations where they could experience anxiety. The environment needs to offer security, consistency and clear boundaries. Nurture groups are ideally able to offer this environment to the children who need it. The emphasis is on routine and repetition: the same people are in the same places at the same time. Nurture groups provide safety and security for the children and also allow the school to respond flexibly to children. It can often seem the case that the rigid structure of a school creates problems for children with emotional and behavioural difficulties. These children lack internalized constraints and need the adults at school to set the boundaries, but the child will have more success if the boundaries have some flexibility. A school that is inflexible limits how the adults can respond to the children. Often the only response to how a child is behaving is a punitive one. However, flexibility does not mean a lowering of expectations of behaviour or achievement. It is essential that nurture group practitioners have high expectations of the children's behaviour and academic achievement, even if the children initially require a high level of support.

Building positive relationships

A vital aspect of a nurture group is to be a place in school where genuine, caring relationships are made between the adults and the children. Many of the children who come to the nurture group find it difficult to build and maintain relationships both with adults and children. They find it hard to accommodate the needs of others; they lack trust and they often see other children or adults as persecutors. They need to have adult role models so they can acquire the skills needed to develop their own caring relationships. Nurture groups provide an environment where relationships can be made that offer the children a sense of safety, acceptance and trust.

Humour

A sense of humour is vital. Nurture groups are about re-parenting and re-creating early family life. A sense of fun, playfulness, humour and gentle teasing should permeate the nurture group. An important aspect of the adults' attitude towards the children is playfulness. Spending time being playful with a child is immensely important and meaningful and can be the start of building a relationship with them.

Self instructional training

Nurture groups allow adults to develop close, positive and affirming attachments with the children. The children feel safe and 'contained' and this can bring about changes in how they perceive themselves and their place in the world around them. The children become more able to regulate their responses to situations previously regarded as very stressful and they start to view themselves as worthwhile individuals. This work is achieved through the relationship with the adults and the structure of the nurture group day, where the days are unhurried and there is a strong routine.

When the children reintegrate with their own classes, even though there can be marked improvements in their self-esteem, their ability to build and sustain relationships and in how well they can manage their responses to difficult situations, there can still be problems in other areas of their lives which limit their chances of success in the class. These can include:

- how well they are able to maintain attention

- being able to sit and listen for periods of time

- following instructions from different adults

- their ability to remain focused on their work.

The child is not deliberately being difficult or defiant, but somehow seems to lack understanding about what they have been asked to do and how to go about it. For example, the class teacher may ask the children to stand up quietly so that they can go to assembly. Some children will stand and wait without talking and will be looking at the teacher listening for the next request. Other children will stand up, but will be whispering to the child next to them, or they may stand up and make straight for the door rather than waiting by their chairs. These children frequently seem to behave impulsively. They act without thinking ahead and their thinking often seems disorganized.

Donald Meichenbaum, in *Cognitive-Behaviour Modification* (1975), describes how we talk to ourselves when we are thinking, solving a problem or learning a new skill. He argues that 'we think and remember with the aid of words which we articulate to ourselves' and that this ability to talk to ourselves is 'instrumental in the logical processing of sensory data'. He suggests that this 'inner speech' is an important part of our thinking process and that it is common to all people.

Meichenbaum argues that there are three stages by which children's behaviour comes under verbal control:

1   Adult talk controls and directs a child's behaviour.

2   The child's own overt speech regulates their behaviour.

3   The child's inner speech 'assumes a self-governing role'.

He goes on to suggest that how much children talk to themselves and the content of what they say is central to developing self-control and the ability to think ahead. He classifies children as either:

- cognitively impulsive: those who respond quickly but who often misunderstand or make mistakes, or

- cognitively reflective: children who take their time and make fewer mistakes.

Cognitively impulsive children's ability to manage themselves whilst at school can be characterized in the following ways (Meichenbaum, 1975):

- They do not always seem able to understand what they are being asked to do.

- They can find it difficult to moderate their behaviour.

- They may have the ability and understanding to manage their behaviour, but fail to do so independently.

- The strategies that such children use to guide their behaviour are not always appropriate. For example, they may copy their friend (but they may also find it hard to stand or line up without talking).

Many of the children in the nurture group display some or more of these tendencies. There is a real need for the children to be taught how to sit, look, listen and take turns. Meichenbaum looked at whether it is possible to work with impulsive children so that they could become more 'cognitively reflective'. He wondered if these children could be taught how to:

- understand what they are being asked to do

- spontaneously produce strategies

- be able to use these strategies to guide and control their behaviour.

Meichenbaum believed that children could be taught to change by helping them to develop their ability to talk to themselves. He developed 'Self Instructional Training' as a process by which children could develop their ability to use self-talk to manage their behaviour.

The self instructional training process

1   The adult performs a task whilst talking to himself out loud

2   The child performs the same task under the direction of the adult's instruction

3   The child performs the task whilst instructing himself aloud

4   The child whispers the instructions to himself as he goes through the task

5   The child performs the task whilst talking silently to himself

(Meichenbaum, 1975)

In the first stage (the adult performs a task whilst talking to himself out loud), it is important that the adult demonstrates particular skills:

- define the problem (*What is it that I have to do?*)

- focus attention (*I need to draw the line carefully; I need to stand very still; I need to walk slowly*)

- positive reinforcement (*Good, I'm doing really well*)

- the ability to correct errors (*I've made a mistake, never mind, I'll just cross it out and carry on*).

It is obvious that this approach may not be appropriate for all children in the nurture group, but certain children may be able to respond positively and be helped to develop important skills so that they are more able to think before they act, maintain attention and be less distracted by what is going on around them. They cope better with frustration and failure, and can control how they behave in different situations.

> I wonder if we are merely rediscovering the potency of reasoning … (The) parent's use of reasoning with their children, in the form of explaining why what the child did was wrong and why he should act in certain ways is related to the child's internalised values, confession upon wrongdoing and resistance to temptation … the type of reasoning used by the parent is the most important antecedent of internalised values and corresponding behaviour. (Meichenbaum, 1975)

Some underlying principles of self instructional training

> Emphasize the need to say aloud what they need to do and how they are going to set about doing it.

> The adult models the behaviours and verbalizes the strategies aloud.

> The adult needs to make deliberate errors and talk aloud about how they will correct themselves.

> Gradually help the child to talk to themselves less loudly.

> Verbalizing the instructions is much more effective than the child reading them silently.

> Asking the child, 'What did you do?' rather than 'Why…' or 'How…' will get more useful answers from the children.

> Children should be shown how to resist temptation, e.g. 'I'm not going to look at (Name) because when I do, I start to laugh.'

How self instructional training worked in Kaleidoscope

The children we worked with had all been in the nurture group for a while and had become more settled and more able to reflect on how they managed school. They were generally Key Stage 2 children, aged eight and nine. This intervention seemed to work best with individual children or pairs of children.

We explained to the children that we were trying to help them with how they behaved in class and that what we were going to work on was their ability to talk to themselves, as this was going to help them change how they responded to situations in the class.

Adults gave the children examples from our own lives of when we talked to ourselves, e.g. when learning to drive a car. Role play or play-acting was very useful; the adults pretended to be the child, and the child pretended to be the teacher.

Some of the children felt embarrassed initially at speaking aloud. Throughout the process we went at the child's pace and didn't try to rush anything.

What did we say?

Following instructions

Now, what does the teacher want me to do? I've got to draw these lines along the dots … I'll go nice and slowly so I don't make a mistake … not too fast … Oh dear, I've gone a bit wrong … never mind, I'll just start that line again, it doesn't matter, I'm doing OK … Keep going nice and slowly … Someone's tapped me on the shoulder … I won't look round, so I can get the work done … Nearly finished … There, I've done really well.

Sitting on the carpet

Now what does my teacher want me to do? … Just sit here quietly … I'm going to keep looking at my teacher so that I'm ready … Someone is tapping me on the shoulder, but I'm not going to look round … I'll just move away a bit and keep looking at my teacher. She has asked a question, I'm going to put my hand up … Oh no, I called out … I mustn't do that … next time I won't call out … I'm sitting really well and I'm not calling out. I've done really well.

Lining up

What do I need to do? … My teacher wants me to line up … so I'll stand up without talking to anybody … I'll keep looking at my teacher so I know what to do … I won't look round at anybody else … someone is whispering my name … I'll just look to see who it is … I must keep looking at my teacher so that I know what to do … Now she wants me to walk to the door … someone has pushed in front of me … It doesn't matter … I am doing the right thing … There, I've lined up … I did really well.

What is important is that the children actually say the words so that they develop their internal speech because this is what will help them. The training involves more than the adults modelling the behaviour.

Managing non-compliance

A significant proportion of children who are placed in a nurture group will have difficulties complying with instructions given by an adult. Non-compliance can be described as happening when a request is made and the child does not begin to make an effort to respond within the first 20 seconds. Often, not only does the child refuse to comply with the request, but they also exhibit negative behaviours that can lead to further difficulties and the original request being forgotten (Kapalka, 2005).

Non-compliance has also been linked with impulsivity. Kapalka argues that 'upon hearing a command to perform a task (one that they would prefer not to do), impulsive children experience an immediate negative reaction to a command ... Impulsive children have difficulties containing that internal reaction and so it becomes immediately translated into oppositional behaviour.'

Managing impulsive and defiant behaviour in the class can be very wearing and can leave the adults frequently worn down and de-skilled. This type of behaviour can lead to several negative outcomes for the teacher and the child (Kapalka, 2005).

- The teacher continues to make the request and the child continues to defy the teacher and this can become a 'loop' which can be repeated several times.

- Teachers can become angry and threatening, but not always following through with the threats, leading to greater non-compliance.

- Teachers can begin to shout, which generally leads to an escalation of the conflict.

It is clear that adults working in schools require a more effective technique when dealing with impulsive children who are non-compliant. The approach that Kapalka recommends was developed by R. A. Barkley in 1997 and it has three parts to it.

1   The teacher issues a request and repeats it once only.

2   If the child refuses to comply with the request, the teacher warns the child of the consequence if they do not comply.

3   The consequence is carried out if the child is still refusing to do what they have been asked.

Kapalka (2005) also argues that to increase the child's compliance, eye contact needs to be held for 20–30 seconds after making the request. Research carried out by him in 2001 shows that 'teachers who minimised repetitions were effective in significantly diminishing non-compliance in the classroom.'

What is clear from Kapalka's work is that if a teacher's approach to non-compliance is simply to continue to repeat a request, becoming more and more angry, this will escalate the conflict, as repeating the request does not stop the impulsive, non-compliant response of the child; rather, the child begins to feel attacked by the teacher and their behaviour is likely to become more defensive. As Kapalka (2005) says, 'When the student and the teacher remain calm, the child is more likely to stop his or her current activity and appropriately process the warning.'

How the brain is affected by trauma and the implications for working with children in nurture groups

Many of the children in nurture groups have experienced relationships based on insecurity, lack of trust, unpredictability and fear. They lack understanding about themselves and other people. They do not seem to know who they are or how to 'be'. They also find it difficult to understand how people around them function and they are slow to trust. Attempts to build relationships with these children can be hard and the adults can often be left feeling de-skilled and unsure what to do.

> The very earliest interpersonal experiences inform the selective development of the neural pathways within the brain … thus consistent, healthy attachment experiences from good enough parents lead to the formation of well organised, well regulated baby brains. (Archer, 2003)

Infants develop the ability to regulate their responses to stress through this close relationship or 'oneness' with the primary caregiver. The importance of this dynamic, two-way, relationship with the parent(s) (the 'dance of attunement') is vital in providing shared experiences through which the infant develops an ability to regulate their own mental and physical states and to manage the change between these states. This close relationship between parent and child has a huge impact on the development of the neural pathways or connections that give the child control over their emotional life (Goleman, 1996). When this relationship is not as it should be, then the child's positive inner working model, their self-esteem, sense of self and self-control do not fully develop, leaving the child finding it hard to deal with traumatic or distressful experiences (Archer, 2003).

Humans have a hierarchy of responses to difficult or threatening situations. The most sophisticated level of response is where reason, logic and language are used to bring understanding and resolution to the problem. The second level is the 'fight or flight' response generated in the limbic system. The most basic level of response, related to the brain stem survival functions (such as breathing and heart rate) is where there is a fall in energy available and the person 'freezes'.

In circumstances where there have been traumatic experiences that have impacted on a child's development, then the child's ability to respond appropriately is severely compromised. In stressful situations, a child is likely to revert to using the more primitive responses outlined above. For such a child, there is a perception of many day-to-day situations being stressful and threatening even when no threat exists.

The traumatized child in the nurture group

Just a low level of stress can trigger the 'fight, flight or freeze' reaction in a child who has been through severe trauma, and they have little control over it (Archer, 2003). The child can experience extreme emotional, physical and mental states that can be overwhelming and out of all proportion to what is actually happening. The child's distorted inner working model will stop him from understanding or recognizing what is going on. He will find it very difficult to be able to learn from it and alter his behaviour and perception of what is happening. Likewise, when these powerful feelings and emotions take over him, it will be very difficult for the child to return to more normal states.

These responses are major barriers to change for children in the nurture group. They may often perceive the nurture group staff as hostile and they will continue to use their poorly adapted survival strategies that have helped them to survive so far. They will find it difficult to alter how they respond and behave and they will continue to rely on 'survival-based behaviours' (Archer, 2003). Nurture group staff can find this behaviour distressing and challenging; it can leave them feeling de-skilled and unclear of what to do.

Implications for nurture group intervention

Nurture groups are a specific intervention for children who have experienced trauma in their early childhood. These children are insecure, slow to trust, and unpredictable.

The origin of these children's difficulties is located in their development in infancy. What they experienced at this stage informs their understanding of what is happening for them now. For these children, what they experience 'continues to be interpreted and processed as though it were in fact still part of the infantile/child's world' (Ayres et al., 2000). Many of the behavioural reactions to events perceived as threatening are what you would expect to see in a much younger child. In fact what is happening is that 'behaviour is not perceived as a direct response to what is occurring objectively, but as related unconsciously to much earlier experience' (Ayres et al., 2000)

Trauma in early childhood can also affect the development of neural pathways in the brain. There tend to be fewer healthy connections between the left and right sides of the brain; connections that are not used, because of poor attachment, tend to decay and are lost. Lack of effective parenting will mean that the child will be unable to regulate itself and lack empathy. He will find it hard to develop a coherent picture of himself. He will be emotionally immature and his view of the world will be distorted (Archer, 2003).

The brain develops from the bottom up (Archer, 2003) so it is vital that work in the nurture group begin at the place where the damage for the children first occurred. For many children, the healing work will begin with the early parent–child relationship, relating to feeling and affect, both internal and external. 'Attempting to intervene at a hierarchically more mature level is analogous to applying mortar to a crumbling building lacking adequate foundations' (Archer, 2003).

Understanding the levels at which the children are functioning

A key principle of nurture group work is that children should be responded to at their developmental rather than actual age. If a child who is six or seven years old is actually functioning as a three-year-old, then this is the age at which the adults in the nurture group should respond to them.

> In Kaleidoscope, we find it very helpful to continually ask ourselves, 'Would we do this with a two-year-old?' It often seems that when things go wrong it is because we are trying to achieve an outcome beyond which the children are capable of managing.

Understanding how attachment develops over the first few years of a child's life enables the adults in the nurture group to select appropriate activities and to structure the day so that the children begin to make progress towards being able to function more successfully at school.

The structure of the nurture group day should be based on 'the attentive, interactive process of mother and child in the earliest years within a structure commensurate with the physical and physiological development of the infant and toddler' (Boxall, 2002). The days should be slow moving, with both adults always near the children and readily available. There is routine and repetition and choices are limited. Resources are chosen that are appropriate for early years play. The adult's speech and how they interact with the children is appropriate for pre-school children.

The emphasis is on the children developing a close relationship with the adults so that they can 'internalise the security that comes from attachment to a reliable, attentive, comforting parent (Boxall, 2002).

How does this attachment develop? Dan Hughes has developed a set of 'Developmental attachment patterns' (Hughes, 1998). Based on the work of Stanley Greenspan, Daniel Stern, Alan Schore and Daniel Siegel, Hughes outlines how normal attachment develops over the child's first four years and gives examples of how the child can become if attachment fails to take place. This list of developmental attachment patterns can be used to identify the stage of development of many of the nurture group children.

> The balance of work in a nurture group should be to providing sensitively attuned responses, nurturing, playfulness and containment that the child did not experience in infancy, in order to replicate the exquisitely synchronised 'dance of attunement' and co-regulation of the mother–infant relationship. (Archer, 2003)

Stages of development and attachment

0–5 months   *Biological regulation*

The parent is aware of the normal patterns of sleeping, feeding and waking and structures the day around this 'biological rhythm' (Hughes, 1998). The emphasis is on food and safety. The needs of the baby are responded to by an attentive parent leading to a 'reciprocal coordination of actions' between child and adult. If this doesn't take place, the child can become either 'disinterested and apathetic or over alert, excited, upset and unfocused.' (Hughes, 1998)

0–12 months   *Attunement*

There is a great deal of eye contact, facial and vocal expressions happening between the adult and the infant. There is a sharing of emotions and much showing of joy and happiness between the infant and the adult. They become increasingly in tune with each other. If this doesn't happen, then the child can become withdrawn and will avoid physical contact and eye contact. Alternatively, the child can become clinging and demanding.

8–18 months   *Behavioural organization*

'A wide range of socially meaningful feelings and behaviours are expressed and organised.' (Hughes, 1998). The child continues to experience and express happiness and interest. They can begin to make choices and act with growing independence but are also happy to accept limits set by parents. The child can begin to control their impulses. If the child does not experience this stage, they can become passive and withdrawn, or experience changes in their moods and how they behave. They demonstrate demanding and stubborn behaviour.

18–36 months   *Thinking and reasoning ability*

Attachment has become internalized. The child is now able to begin to use words to express feelings, desires and intentions. Their use of language is increasingly organized. They are able to reflect on their actions. If the child does not go through this stage, then their vocabulary can be limited, and they can find it hard to talk about how they are feeling, or their talk can be made up of 'disorganised, fragmented chatter.' (Hughes,1998)

30–48 months   *Narrative building*

The child is able to use an increasingly sophisticated vocabulary to 'relate to others across a wide range of emotions and ideas, forming a coherent autobiographical narrative.' (Hughes, 1998).The child knows about himself and can express this. There is a growing awareness of how he affects others and how people around him affect him. If the child does not go through this stage, then he can be more withdrawn and find it hard to talk about what he is feeling. The child can also find it difficult to maintain focus and direction.

Key ideas

> We need to be clear what we are looking for when selecting children for the nurture group. Nurture groups are a specific intervention for children whose difficulties are related to stress and adversity that has impacted on the nurturing process of their earliest years.

> The Boxall Profile is the key assessment tool for nurture group practitioners. Use of the Profile enables the adults to begin to see the world through the child's eyes and work empathically.

> There are many approaches to working with children in the nurture group that are helpful. John Visser outlines 'eternal verities' that he believes should be present to ensure effective practice when working with children who have emotional and behavioural difficulties.

> Understanding how the brain can be affected by trauma and the implications this has for how well children can manage at school, and how adults can support them, is very important for nurture group practitioners.

> A key principle of nurture group work is to recognize at what developmental stage the children are functioning and to take them on from there.

Further reading

Boxall, M. (2002) *Nurture Groups in Schools: Principles and Practice*. London: Paul Chapman.

Hughes, D. (1998) *Building the Bonds of Attachment: Awakening Love in Deeply Troubled Children*. Northville, NJ: Jason Aronson.

Bennathan, M and Boxall, M. (1998) *The Boxall Profile, Handbook for Teachers.* Maidstone: Nurture Group Network.

Goleman, D. (1996) *Emotional Intelligence: Why It Can Matter More Than IQ*. London: Bloomsbury.

Goldberg, S. (2000) *Attachment and Development*. London: Arnold.

4

How to Run a Nurture Group Effectively

This chapter covers

> a typical day in a nurture group
> the role of the adults in the nurture group
> behaviour management
> reintegrating children into their mainstream classes
> working with parents
> working with other professionals.

The aim of the nurture group staff is to create the type of day that would be 'equivalent to the first three years at home' (Boxall, 2002). There is much routine and repetition – same people, same places, same times. The children are accepted at whatever emotional level they are operating, regardless of their chronological age. What should be seen in the nurture group is the type of learning you would expect to see in pre-school years, from birth to three years (Boxall, 2002). The week is structured so that each day is slow moving and carefully controlled. Tasks are short and achievable so that the children experience success. The structure of the day lets the children know that they are safe and secure and they can begin to learn, develop and grow.

The timetable below is not prescriptive. It is the timetable that has evolved over time in Kaleidoscope. It is important for nurture group staff to continue to reflect on and modify their timetables as necessary. In Kaleidoscope we have worked with children aged five to nine years old.

A typical day in a nurture group

Daily Timetable								
9.00–9.40	9.40–10.10 Breakfast	10.15–10.30 Assembly	10.30–10.45 Playtime	10.45–12.15 Free choice activities **Literacy** **Maths**	12.15–1.15 Lunch	1.15–1.30 Reading	1.30–2.30	2.30–3.15
Register Showing What are we doing today? Action songs Preparing for breakfast				Literacy activities 11.05–11.20 Free choice activities 11.20–11.40 Numeracy activities Free choice activities 11.55–12.05 Tidying away 12.05–12.10 Circle Time activities			Mondays Games outside Tuesdays Art activities Wednesday Trip to shops for ingredients Thursdays Cooking Friday In classes	KS 1 Children out to play and back to class KS 2 Children return to class at 2.45

The Kaleidoscope day

9.00–9.10   The day begins with the children being registered in their own classes. This is in line with the classic Boxall Model where the children maintain links with their own classes. Time in the class is important to the development of the relationship between the child and the class teacher, making successful reintegration more achievable. It is also important that the class teacher deals with behaviour issues that may occur at registration times. The danger is that nurture group staff are the only adults to manage a child's behaviour in school and other teachers can become anxious about how they will cope with the child when they are reintegrated. Kaleidoscope staff collect the children and bring them to the nurture group room. We have found it very important to have the same people in the same places at the same time. Some children need us to be waiting in class to welcome them when they arrive and help them to settle and get ready for the class teacher.

9.10–9.30   We have two rooms in Kaleidoscope and we always begin the day in the smaller room where the children and adults can sit on large comfortable floor cushions. We have our own register where the children's photographs are put into coloured holders and we can see who is here and who is away. This is an opportunity for counting and working out simple number problems. We work out what the day and the date are, what the weather is like and we discuss what we are doing that day. Some of the children in the nurture group benefit from having the activities of the day shown visually, in the form of photographs. Once we have completed these activities, we have a time enjoying action songs. What helps this time to be successful is to always start with the same two or three songs and only introduce new ones gradually. The children respond to the familiarity of their favourite tunes.

9.30–10.00   Breakfast! We sit at the table and sort out our place names, mats, plates, cups and cutlery. Place mats can be different shapes, colours and sizes, which allows for plenty of language development. This is the same with giving out the plates and cups. The children decide whether they would like juice or tea to drink, with different children taking turns to gather this information. Children take turns with simple jobs such as giving the toast out, or pouring the juice. We all help each other. There is plenty of opportunity to practise speaking and listening skills throughout breakfast. The adults are able to chat to each other, with the children listening; the children chat to each other and the adults. There is laughter and serious issues to talk about, just as there should be over any mealtime. The children take turns to clear the table and to help with washing up. Rotas are important, so that the children can see that everything is fair.

10.00–10.15   Just before assembly we play board games, such as snakes and ladders or Scaredy Cat, or Incy Wincy Spider. We sometimes play matching games or bingo.

10.15–10.45   The children return to their classes for assembly. Nurture group staff sit near them if we know that a child finds this time stressful. The children go out to play with their classes. Nurture group staff are in the playground to be a familiar face if needed.

10.45–12.15   This is the part of the day when the children undertake more academic work. The tasks are always kept short and achievable, so that the children can finish them and experience success. The work is broken up with time for 'choosing'. These times help the child to focus on their work, and complete their tasks, because they do not want to miss out on their play activity. It is up to individual nurture group practitioners to decide on the content of the academic work, but it is important to remember that nurture groups are recreating the earliest learning experiences of the first three years. Within Kaleidoscope, we experience success during this part of the day if we ask ourselves, 'would we do this with a two- or three-year-old?' When problems occur, it can often be because we are asking too much of the children.

During this part of the day we practise the children's skills of functioning as part of a group. These would include:

- Taking turns and waiting for their turn

- Putting their hand up when they wish to speak

- Asking for help

- Developing good speaking and listening skills, e.g. eye contact

- Practising strategies that will help them cope with situations they find stressful in the classroom.

Some children go out with other members of staff during this time. They might take part in activities that support their reading or speaking and listening skills. They may be involved in outdoor activities (Forest School) or it might be their turn to read. Involving other adults from around the school is very helpful for nurture group children.

We tidy up and gather together just before lunch for a short circle time activity where we hand round a 'speaking object' and talk about what we have enjoyed that morning. The children are encouraged to wait until they can see the other children are looking and listening before they speak. The adults remind the children about the afternoon activities and then take the children back to their classes for lunch.

1.15–1.30   The children are collected from their classes and we read stories together sitting on our floor cushions. This is also a time when the children can talk about how lunchtime went for them.

1.30–2.30   Each day of the week has its own afternoon activity. This helps the children to feel secure about school and to have a growing awareness and confidence about school. The children quite quickly remember which activity happens on which day.

Monday: Games outside such as Hide and Seek, What's the time Mr. Wolf?, Granny's Footsteps, The Farmer's in his Den, and so on. If it rains we play games inside, such as Twister, and Sleeping Lions.

Tuesday: We have an art afternoon, which is usually linked to the book we are reading for our literacy activities. If we were reading an Elmer story we might make clay elephants in the afternoon.

Wednesday: This is the day when we go to the shops to buy ingredients for the cooking activity. We look through our recipe books and decide what we want to cook. The children write a list and we count out our money. 'Real-life' trips such as to the shops are very valuable. Children have to make real choices, take responsibility for what they choose, walk safely, behave well in the shops and carry the shopping back to school. If it is fine weather, and there is time, we may go to the park quickly on the way back.

Thursday: Cooking: this is a fantastic activity to do with the children – so much learning goes on and so much fun is had. The children love taking what they have cooked to various members of staff, and there is a lovely 'family feel' about these afternoons.

Friday: The children go back to their classes in the afternoon so that Kaleidoscope staff have non-contact time. In the morning, we go to a local Toy Library run by NCH, where the children are able to borrow toys and bring them back to school. Again, this is a fantastic 'real-life' experience that is so valuable for the children. They take responsibility for the toy they borrow and have to look after it. They have to be aware of the other children using the Toy Library. They have to walk safely and they have to carry the toy they borrow. If it is too heavy, they need to be able to ask another child or an adult to help them carry it. On the way back we stop to play at the park if it is fine.

2.30–3.15   The children go out to play and back to their classes for the last session of the day. This is so that the child keeps building the relationship with his peers and the class teacher. If the child needs support, then an adult from the nurture group will stay to ensure that this time can be managed.

Applying this to your own setting

What we have tried to create with this timetable are days that are 'slow moving and routinised' (Boxall, 2002). The activities are 'basic, clearly delineated, frequently repeated and carefully planned and controlled'. For the children there is clear order and clear routines. Much of what happens is repetitive and the children become very familiar with what is happening each day in the nurture group.

> The situation is made appropriate for an earlier developmental level; simpler, more immediate, more routinised, more protected. Restrictions and constraints provide clarity of experience and focus the child's attention; he engages at his level, his attention is held and there is much repetition. Basic experiences and attachment to the adult are consolidated. The child experiences satisfaction and approval and attachment is strengthened. Routine gives security and he anticipates with confidence and pleasure. (Boxall, 2002)

Each nurture group will develop its own timetable based on the principles outlined by Marjorie Boxall. The Kaleidoscope model is not prescriptive. One of the strengths of the nurture group is that much of the work is intuitive and each group will build on the strengths of their own practitioners. The challenge for practitioners starting up a new nurture group is to ensure that the whole school understands that it offers something different to what will be seen in a mainstream class. The aims of the nurture group teacher and assistant are different from that of a class teacher and the practice will be different. 'It is crucial that the children become attached. Their needs then become apparent and the teacher and assistant respond accordingly. The learning process follows' (Boxall, 2002). However the timetable is structured and whatever resources are used, time must be given for attachments to develop between the adults and the children. This is the basis of the work. This is how progress is made, and this is how children develop.

The role of the adults

The relationship that develops between the children and the adults is central to the work in a nurture group. The adults have to be able to create an environment where the children feel safe and secure. Within this environment the adults are able to act as 'containers' for the children's unsettling feelings. The adults have to understand and feel to some degree what the children are experiencing and reflect it back to them in a way that the children can cope with. Over time, how the children see themselves and how they perceive stressful situations begins to change, and they respond less defensively. This can often be challenging for the adults running the nurture group because it can be difficult to understand what is happening for the children; how they respond to different situations can be unpredictable.

Most of the children who are placed in nurture groups come from backgrounds where their early nurturing needs have not been met. There is a whole range of factors that can impinge on parents' ability to provide this care. These can include:

- homelessness

- lengthy illness

- poverty and poor housing

- physical or mental illness

- physical, emotional or sexual abuse

- alcohol or drug problems

- bereavement

- difficulties with learning

- family breakdown

- inconsistent parenting approaches.

Many children are affected by more than one of these factors. Sometimes the difficulties that they and their families face seem overwhelming and we wonder how they can function at all. These children bring their pain, confusion, damage and their ways of managing their difficulties with them into the nurture group and the adults' task is to form a relationship that enables change to happen and the child to grow.

In Chapter 3 we looked at the work of Dan Hughes and the attitude of the adults towards children. Adults should develop an attitude towards the children which is (Hughes, 1998):

1   accepting

2   curious

3   empathetic

4   loving

5   playful.

Frequently, the children that we are working with can make it difficult to maintain this attitude. They can behave in very challenging ways. Working with children who have emotional and behavioural difficulties can be very wearing. The adults can frequently be left feeling worn down and de-skilled and they can question the effectiveness of the work that they are doing and the achievements that have been made. In Chapter 2, we established two sets of principles:

1   To facilitate the capacity for fun and love

2   To facilitate effective discipline.

These principles are very useful to keep in mind when behaviour becomes very challenging. The adults in the nurture group benefit from reflecting on their practice and how situations are managed. Having principles to refer to can help to ensure that practice is positive and give practitioners confidence.

How does this work in Kaleidoscope?

At the forefront of each day is the building and maintaining of positive relationships with the children using these principles to guide how the adults relate to the children. Many of the elements on Dan Hughes' list are to do with a very close interaction with the child. There is physical contact between adults and children as well as sharing of activities and thoughts. We create feelings of closeness and togetherness through the use of eye contact, smiles, touch, hugs and humour.

Dan Hughes also emphasizes the concept of attunement, and there need to be many opportunities when the children can experience attunement with the adults. There was a 'breakthrough moment' with a particular child during breakfast. This was a child who was highly anxious within the classroom setting and would relate only minimally to other children and adults at school. He was sitting at the breakfast table with his chin resting on his hand, waiting for his toast. He looked up and saw that one of the adults was imitating him. He moved his hand to his cheek; so did the adult. He moved his hand to the top of his head; so did the adult. A beautiful smile broke over this child's face as he realized the game that was being played. This game was played several times a day over several weeks, with sometimes the adult leading and sometimes the child. It didn't work if the adult tried to make the child play. This interaction needs to be spontaneous and natural. For this child, there was a dramatic drop in behaviours reflecting high levels of anxiety at school. He was able to sit next to visitors to the nurture group and chat with them. He became more able to talk to adults around the school and his play moved on from being isolated and repetitive, to him being able to interact with a variety of children in different roles.

Games are played where adults and child can experience fun and enjoyment. There is imaginative role-play where the adults are following the children's lead. There are cushions to sit on so that children and adults can cuddle up and enjoy sharing books and videos together. The children also enjoy listening to the adults talking about their own lives and families. Children's birthdays are celebrated: we always make cakes and have a party. We have routines that lead to the development of our shared history. We are able to look back together and also think about the future. There is often music playing and the children and adults will dance and sing along. There is also the flexibility to be able to spend quiet times with the children when they may be feeling worried or finding a situation stressful.

We have also found that staying physically close to the children is vital in maintaining a calm, safe environment. One child who came to the nurture group had been described as 'a monster' by his previous school because of his disruptive behaviour; he only attended school for half an hour each day. He was aggressive and would hit out at both adults and children. He would frequently swear. Spitting was an issue. He was defiant and would refuse to comply with the teacher's requests. Many members of staff were wary of him because of his aggression and so would keep a safe distance from him. When he was placed in Kaleidoscope, we decided that we would follow Dan Hughes' principles of staying physically close to him and making choices for him. For the first few weeks, he was only able to do a limited range of activities and one of us was always very close to him. We had a great deal of bad language from him, and we decided that rather than just telling him 'not to swear', we would tell him which words he couldn't say. So we had conversations where we would say, 'You can't say —. You mustn't say — at school.'

He would reply, 'I can't say —? Will I get into trouble?'

We would tell him that he would get into trouble if he said — . He would ponder this and generally accept what we had told him. We felt that he hadn't really understood what adults had meant by 'Don't swear' and he needed to know the actual words. We were also very clear about providing 'natural and logical consequences for (his) behaviours' (Hughes, 2000). We found that sitting him in a separate room with a five-minute egg timer was extremely effective. When he swore, or was aggressive or defiant, he would have five minutes' time out, and we would make it very clear to him that we were continuing to have a lovely time with the other children which he was missing. We would not start the egg timer until he was calm and initially he could take up to twenty minutes before we could start the egg timer. We found that staying close to him really helped to reduce his aggression as well. In fact through observing him in his class, it seemed clear that he felt school quite an overwhelming place and often appeared confused and anxious. With an adult nearby reminding and prompting him, he became much more relaxed and able to manage his own behaviour. It became apparent that the close proximity of trusted adults led to a lessening of his perceptions of certain situations being stressful. When the adult is in this role, they are 'leading' the child and ensuring that the child is functioning within boundaries. The adult is also 'one step ahead', and is always 'attuned to the affect of your child' (Hughes, 2000) and aware of the possibilities of what might happen, so that they are able to respond proactively rather than reactively.

Behaviour management

There are five aspects of behaviour management that we will deal with here.

1   the structure and content of the day

2   the balance of the group

3   the adults' attitude towards the children

4   sanctions

5   working as part of a team: support for the adults.

The structure and content of the day

The structure, routine and repetition of a typical nurture group day plays a large part in supporting the adults in managing the children's behaviour. For many children, being in a nurture group removes them from the types of situation that can trigger behaviour problems:

- the stress of being in a large group

- the feeling that they are not liked by adults and/or other children

- not being able to tolerate frustrations in their work.

As soon as the children are placed in the nurture group it is not uncommon to see a reduction in difficult behaviour. The days are more predictable and slow moving, the children are experiencing success, pressure is taken off them and adults respond to them at their functional level. The structure of the day allows for a balance of support and challenge for the children. The children actually enjoy the activities and *want* to be part of the group.

The balance of the group

It is very important to ensure that there is the right mix of children: there must be careful selection to ensure that the group can function. If the balance of the group is weighted too much in favour of children with severe behavioural problems, then it will not be possible to create the nurturing atmosphere required. The group needs to be set up so that it can succeed.

The adults' attitude towards the children

The adults' attitude towards the children in the nurture group is so important. It can be summarized (Hughes, 1998) as playful, loving, accepting, curious and empathetic. It is vital that the adults in the nurture group set the emotional tone of the interactions with the children (Hughes, 1998). The children need to be provided with many experiences where they are able to experience being 'in tune' with the adults. These experiences will involve eye contact, smiles, humour, surprises, touch and movement. These experiences need to happen to replicate the 'dance of attunement' of the mother–infant relationship (Archer, 2003).

Sanctions

Part of the adults' role is to be a mental container for the children's feelings and emotions. The adults need to feel what the child is feeling and hold it for them whilst reflecting it back to the child in a manageable way. For this to happen effectively, there need to be effective sanctions in place that 'give strength to the sides of the container'. Sanctions are effective when they are consistently applied, but not punitive; rather they 'have to be perceived by the pupils as an irritating inconvenience' (Craig, 2005). An effective sanction is where the children are removed from the group to spend some time alone (time out). It is very useful if there is a second room within the nurture group where the child can be so that other children aren't disturbed. Failing that, a place needs to be specified, such as the sofa, or a particular chair or cushion. A five-minute egg timer is used so that the child can see the time passing and knows that the sanction is manageable. However, the timer is not started until the child is calm. This means that the child can be out of the room for considerably longer than five minutes (Sylva and Lunt, 1982). An alternative to this is 'time in': the child is taken away from the difficult situation sits with an adult, using the egg timer, when the child is calm. There needs to be a period of 'reattunement' between adult and child following these episodes.

Working as part of a team: support for the adults

The children and families with whom the staff work can be difficult to understand and manage. Adults working within a nurture group can feel isolated, worn down and uncertain about a direction to take with particular children. It is essential that nurture group staff work as part of a team, so that they are able to have time to share and reflect on the relationships in the nurture group. The adults need a secure base that is 'the emotional and physical refuge in which uncertainties are processed into thoughts and the base from which exploration can take place' (Geddes, 2006).

In her book *Attachment in the Classroom* Heather Geddes suggests a 'work discussion group' as a useful way forward in providing supervision and support for teachers. This is where a group of adults commit to meeting regularly. A member of the group presents a situation that is causing anxiety or difficulties, and the group ask questions, reflect on the situation presented and suggest ways forward based on a shared, deeper understanding. This forum can become the 'secure thinking base within the school' (Geddes, 2006).

Reintegrating children into their mainstream classes

This can be one of the trickiest aspects of nurture group work to get right. Reintegration should begin when the child has been managing well in the nurture group and around the school for a period of time and has been judged by the adults as being ready to go back to their class. Often the child will begin to really *want* to go back and will ask if they can work in their own class. Another sign is that they may seem bored with the routine of the nurture group. The child will also have shown that they can cope well for the parts of the day where they are back with their teacher.

Marjorie Boxall in *Nurture Groups in School: Principles and Practice* (2002: 211–16) goes into detail about the process of reintegration and the need for communication and flexibility between everyone involved. Much discussion and planning is needed for reintegration to be successful, and relationships need to be built between the child and the receiving teacher. Sometimes the nurture group child might develop a close relationship with another adult in the class and this person can support the reintegration process. There also needs to be time given to the child developing relationships with their peers. Issues of furniture, space and classroom equipment all need to be addressed so that the child feels part of the class.

Working with parents

The relationship with the parents is very important and needs to be developed and encouraged by the nurture group staff. There needs to be:

- empathy and understanding: seeing the situation through the parents' eyes

- a non-judgemental attitude towards the parents

- transparency of communication

- clarity about the work of the nurture group

- consistency

- confidentiality.

When the parents are initially approached about considering whether their child could be part of the nurture group, it can be helpful for a teacher with whom they have a good relationship to talk with them first. This teacher can support the parents when they meet with the nurture group staff.

There are many opportunities for informal talks with the parents at the beginning or end of the day. There also need to be regular meetings where the child's progress can be discussed in a more formal setting.

Children seem to be able to make most progress when the parents are given time to reflect on the relationship between themselves and their child and how they might

Policy for the reintegration of nurture group children to their mainstream classes

1 Purpose

We intend to help all children attain the highest level of achievement of which they are capable and to be able to function successfully within their mainstream class. This will require a balance of nurture group activities within the nurture group and the children attending a growing number of carefully selected lessons or activities within their mainstream classes. A systematic and planned approach is required. The teaching staff, classroom assistants and nurture group staff need to work in partnership to ensure that the needs of the children are met throughout this process and ensure that parents have a clear understanding about the reintegration process.

2 Broad guidelines

- The nurture group staff will use a variety of assessments to ensure that children's needs are being met and that they are moving towards reintegration as appropriate.

- When the child is assessed as being ready to be reintegrated to their class an initial meeting will be set up with the class teacher and other key adults so that a reintegration programme can be planned and instigated.

- Parents will be kept fully informed so that they are able to offer support and discuss any concerns.

- Appropriate lessons/activities, timings and key adults will be discussed and agreed.

- All staff will need to be aware of rewards/sanctions that can be used.

- All staff need to be aware of issues such as furniture and equipment for the child.

- Time will need to be given to developing relationships between the child and key adults through activities such as breakfast in the nurture group.

- Kaleidoscope staff and class teacher to plan appropriate activities as required.

- Reintegration to be completed over a two- to six-week timetable.

3 Plan for implementation

- Nurture group staff to organise, carry out and record appropriate assessments.

- Initial discussions between nurture group staff, class teacher and classroom assistants concerning activities/lessons which the child can continue to take part in within the mainstream class to ensure contact is not lost.

- Nurture group staff to meet with parents to discuss aims of reintegration.

- Head teacher kept fully informed.

work at overcoming issues and difficulties they might have. If parents raise issues about their own lives or situations, it may be more appropriate to make use of other professionals who can then work with the parents. Schools are increasingly buying into services so that parents can be offered support from trained counsellors and therapists who can work either with the family or individually.

However, it is important that nurture group staff are able to discuss the child's progress and also able to offer support and advice when appropriate. There is a range of assessments and resources that can be used to bring together the views of the parents and the views of the teachers and establish a common ground from which progress can be made.

Interviews

A semi-structured interview might include these questions:

1   Can you tell me a little about your child?

2   How does he get on at school/home?

3   What do you think is the main problem?

4   Has he always had some difficulties?

5   Has he had any help?

6   How do you feel about him attending the nurture group?

7   Is there anything else you would like to tell me?

A solution-focused approach

The children who are placed in the nurture group have complex needs and difficulties. Parents often want to help their children but are unsure where to start. 'Solution-focused brief therapy' (Long and Fogell, 1999) is an approach which helps parents and adults to focus on one or two areas of concern and to 'identify solutions which are within the grasp of individuals'. Adults set priorities and choose targets with which they can experience success.

1   The first stage in this process is to work with the parents to identify the major concerns that they have about their situation. This list should not be too long, Long and Fogell (1999) suggest a maximum of five problems.

2   The next stage is for the parents to think of a solution to each of the problems. The parents need to think about how they would like the situation to be if the problem did not exist. The parents are being asked to imagine an ideal future: how they would like the situation to be if the current problems were removed. The discussion about the ideal future needs to focus on a possible situation

that is realistic and achievable. 'The aim … is to help clients to identify their personal resources to work towards solutions … false or inappropriate goals [must] be avoided' (Long and Fogell, 1999).

3   Having thought through solutions, the parents now need to see if they could begin to resolve any of the identified problems. For some parents, it may be that they have identified some situations that seem irresolvable and it may be appropriate to ask the parents to consider additional support through other professionals such as Health or Social Services. Hopefully there will be one or two situations that the parents feel that the child could make some progress towards resolving. At this stage, it is useful to identify where parents think the child is are on a scale of 1 to 10, with 1 being no progress made and 10 being the goal being reached. The parents can then think of progress being in small steps towards their goals as opposed to resolving the whole situation immediately.

4   The final stage of this process is to identify the short-term targets that allow the parents and the child to begin to move towards their goals and to list the people or resources that will help them.

Working with other professionals

Nurture groups become more effective when a range of other professionals are involved who can offer a wider range of support to families and children. These might include Social Services, family workers, Health Visitors, school nurses, paediatricians, educational psychologists and CAMHS teams. Some of these professionals can be part of the steering group and have input through that forum; others may work more regularly with the nurture group staff supporting children and families.

How this works in Kaleidoscope

The areas where we have found it important to offer support through other professionals are:

• Supporting parents who feel isolated and without anyone to turn to for help

• Working with the parents on developing children's routines and boundaries

• Helping parents to focus on positive reinforcement and the importance of play

• Working with individual children and offering an opportunity for counselling to try to help them to better understand and manage their emotions.

We work closely with two services to help with these areas. They are:

• NCH, who have worked with the school to set up a project called 'the Quiet Place' where children are offered individual time once a week; and

- Family Advice Liaison Workers, who work with the whole family, offering ongoing advice and support. The FALWs also put families in contact with other support services who might be more able to meet the needs of the family.

We meet termly with the FALW and the Quiet Place worker to discuss children or families who might benefit from this extra input. There are also informal discussions about concerns that might arise from week to week.

Not all families require this extra support. For many, just the intervention of the nurture group is enough, but for the families or children who do need more, then it has been very effective to be able to offer the support outlined above.

Key ideas

> The structure of the day is very important. The timetable should be organized so that there is a great deal of routine and repetition with 'the same people in the same places at the same time'.

> Clear and unhurried routines help a great deal in managing children's behaviour. It is also vital to get the balance of the group right. A group full of 'acting out' children will be impossible to manage, as would a group of children who are very withdrawn.

> Clear sanctions must be in place and implemented consistently to ensure that the nurture group is a safe place to be for the children where they feel 'contained'. Each nurture group will need to evolve its own set of sanctions.

> Reintegration can be difficult for some nurture group children. It may be that they will continue to require adult support in the class. Planning for reintegration needs to happen well in advance of the child going back to their class.

> There will be both formal and informal meetings with parents.

> Some of the difficulties that families are experiencing are beyond the remit of the nurture group staff, and it is important that there are good contacts with other professionals who are better placed to offer the right type of support to the families.

Further reading

Long, R. and Fogell, J. (1999) *Supporting Pupils with Emotional Difficulties: Creating a Caring Environment for All*. London: David Fulton.

Sylva, K. and Lunt, I. (1982) *Child Development: A First Course*. Oxford: Basil Blackwell.

5

Keeping on Course

Team working and asking for help

Children who are placed in the nurture group can display a range of very challenging behaviour that can be hard for the adults to understand and manage. It can be difficult to respond positively and with understanding day after day. The adults can feel 'de-skilled, angry, despairing, anxious, depressed or isolated' (Ayers et al., 2000).

Throughout the school day there are many opportunities for situations to arise that can raise stress levels, and anxiety can trigger behaviour problems for the children. There are three common problem areas:

- The learning situation: difficulties can arise through making mistakes, lack of confidence, not being able to persevere, not being able to deal with frustrations, not knowing what to do.

- Coping with peers: difficulties can arise when the child finds it harder than others to learn and grasp new skills and concepts; children can feel left out and unwanted by others.

- Relationship with the teacher: enormous demands are made of teachers dealing with children with emotional and behavioural difficulties and the relationship can often be strained.

Paul Greenhalgh in *Emotional Growth and Learning* (1994) describes the feelings adults can have when working with children who have emotional and behavioural difficulties. 'It is not just a question of feeling drained each day – the feelings are often much more precise and intense than that.' He describes how the adults can feel 'hurt, abused, angry, frustrated, intolerant, anxious, de-skilled and even frightened'. It is not always clear to the adults why they are experiencing these powerful feelings or where they originate. This can be the process of 'projection', an 'unconscious process by which feelings get pushed out and onto other things' (Greenhalgh, 1994). When projection occurs, there is a 'sense of release' for that person. If it is the teacher onto whom the feelings are being projected, then they can end up with 'the intolerable feeling which really belongs to the child in difficulty'. Projection is a defence mechanism that we all use. To varying degrees, we are able to recognize when we use it and can try not to project our feelings onto others. However, many of the children in the nurture group are 'without the inner resources to tolerate a difficult feeling, a capacity for reflection and the language to communicate' (Greenhalgh, 1994) and so are more likely to 'express the difficult feeling through unconsciously "acting it out" thus making others have the feelings associated with the difficulty' (Greenhalgh, 1994).

'Transference' is one form of projection that occurs when 'feelings from the past, or emotions one has about someone significant are unconsciously transferred onto another person' (Greenhalgh, 1994). For the teacher it can be as though the problems associated with someone else (usually the parents) are transferred to him or her.

What we can begin to understand is that 'the relationship between teacher and pupil is fraught with meaning. It is a relationship which is imbued with attachment significance and affected by unconscious processes' (Geddes, 2006). The adults will also be bringing their own 'unconscious processes' to the relationship and the way they react can exacerbate problems. The adults can find that they are somehow re-enacting the same negative interactions with the child day after day.

When a school is considering opening a nurture group, thought must be given to how the staff running it will be supported. Unless there is appropriate support for the staff working with these children, then the teachers themselves can become worn down, their confidence sapped and they 'can become reactive and respond with rejection, criticism and punishment' (Geddes, 2006).

It can feel to the adults as though they are having to battle on 'without the professional and emotional support which they could receive from those with special expertise' (Hanko, 1995).

How schools can support nurture group staff

Teachers require a combination of both professional and emotional support to enable them to support children with emotional and behavioural difficulties. Time is needed for reflection. Paul Greenhalgh (1994) suggests that 'the dynamics involved in working with emotional/behavioural issues can become confusing, and the perspective derived from consulting with another person can be of significant benefit.' He goes on to argue that schools need to develop a framework that can allow joint problem solving and consultation to take place. Teachers should have opportunities to consider particular children or situations together, the aim being to clarify issues and to solve problems. Gerda Hanko (1995) defines consultation as a process within which three tasks can take place. These tasks include:

1   generating relevant information

2   enabling the teacher to make decisions about what to do next

3   helping the teacher to implement changes and/or interventions.

The process should be carried out in an atmosphere where the adults involved 'can work together as professionals with equal but differing expertise, engaged in a process of joint exploration which seeks to develop ... professional understanding and skills concerning ... the pupils' (Hanko, 1995). For this to happen, the group requires a consultant. For most schools, someone on the staff team would take this role, but it would probably not be the head teacher. Their role is that of an 'informed facilitator'. They are not there to be a 'judge, assessor or supervisor of the consultees' performance', but rather to 'extend the teachers' understanding of children's behaviour, its effects and treatment and the significance of the teachers' part in dealing with it' (Hanko, 1995).

Within the consultation time there will be a focus on:

•   the child's situation and how they manage their behaviour

•   how the teacher perceives and understands the situation

•   how the teacher is affected by the situation with the child, e.g. loss of confidence

•   highlighting the issues 'in an enabling way which points towards workable alternatives' rather than prescribing what to do (Hanko, 1995).

The aim of the consultation process should be to:

•   enable a reduction in anxiety about a child

•   develop a better understanding about the situation with the child

•   arrive at possible solutions.

'The process of joint exploration ... is utilised to enable teachers to redirect their perceptions and to answer for themselves the questions raised in the exploration rather than having them answered for them' (Hanko, 1995).

Organizing the consultation meeting

Each session will focus on a particular child.

Stage One

The first part of the consultation process is where the adult shares information about the child. This information will cover three main areas (Hanko, 1995):

1   understanding the child and the underlying issues that have led to the difficulties that have developed and how the child manages stress and anxiety at school

2   understanding how the child relates to the rest of the class and what their particular difficulties might be in relation to being part of a large group

3   understanding the relationship between the child and the adult. this will include developing a greater awareness of what is personally significant for the adult.

The adult will also outline what strategies have already been tried with the child and how successful these strategies have been.

Stage Two

The second part of the process is where there is a time for reflection and 'restoring objectivity' (Hanko, 1995). Where an adult is working with a child who has emotional and behavioural difficulties, it can be hard to keep personal feelings from intruding into the situation. This can mean that the adult can misunderstand or misjudge interactions with the child. They can over-react to, or avoid, difficult situations, or be affected by their own beliefs or experiences about children, schools and family (Hanko, 1995). Paul Greenhalgh (1994) suggests that the consultant should enable the group to reflect on 'how the feelings of those involved relate to their capacities to find and use effective strategies'.

This will also be the opportunity for members of the group to share any additional information that might be relevant that will help to shed light on the child's situation.

Stage Three

The third part of this process is where the consultant guides the group towards developing strategies that can lead to problems being resolved. Hanko (1995) suggests that there are three strands to this process.

1   The ability to see beyond the behaviour displayed. The group will spend time thinking about the needs of the child, which may at present be covered up by their behaviour. Observation, assessment and time to consider all will help this process.

2   Developing 'special bridging efforts' (Hanko, 1995). This is where the adult is helped by the consultation process to understand the child and the situation from a different perspective. It can be that the adult's understanding of the meaning behind a situation needs to change, so that the actions of the child can be interpreted from a fresh perspective:

>   The teacher needs to be able to perceive and to build on what is good in a child, to listen and to share his experience without intruding, to express acceptance and to convey to the child unostentatiously that his words and acts are understood as signs of the child's anxiety. (Hanko, 1995)

3   The third strand in this process is to look at how the school day can be structured in such a way that the child is able to experience success. This is where the staff will need to think of particular 'triggers' that may provoke a variety of feelings for the child. These might be to do with people, changes, peers, academic work, or unstructured parts of the day. Getting this right will 'help to amend the limiting ideas that the child may have developed about himself in relation to others and to the tasks he has been set' (Hanko, 1995).

Behaviour plans and the most challenging children

There are a variety of ways that behaviour is managed in the nurture group. As we have seen, there is much reliance on the structure of the day, two adults working together, the size of the group, and routine and repetition.

However, some children will still find it too difficult to manage for the whole day and it can be that they display aggressive and disruptive behaviour that impacts negatively on the whole group. Marjorie Boxall (2002) argues that where this is the case 'behaviour control is an urgent priority and is strict and unremitting at all times … It is through the adults unremitting control and the consistency and immediacy of their response, within a context of fairness and caring that the children learn to trust and become attached, dependable and biddable.'

Many of the children in the nurture group respond to firm and clear boundaries and indeed often can be seen to relax in the nurture group, because they know the adults are in charge. However, there are some children who find it very difficult to control their feelings and emotions. This inability to regulate their responses to situations that they find stressful can often end in outbursts of temper, which can be severe. Temper tantrums are usually triggered by frustration and are 'characterized by rage' (Boxall, 2002). The child may be lashing out at people or property around them and they may not be able to control themselves.

Physical restraint

If this situation arises, then Marjorie Boxall (2002) states that 'it is important that a child in a tantrum is held, and continues to be held.' The primary reason for holding a child who is out of control is 'because he needs to be physically contained when emotionally in disorder ... the aim is to constrain, limit and channel his aggression'. Situations like these can very quickly arise in the nurture group and it is important that the nurture group staff are confident enough to ensure that the situation is made safe for the child concerned and the rest of the group.

It is of vital importance in this situation is that the adults are acting lawfully. .

Section 550A of the Education Act 1996 states:

A member of the staff of a school may use, in relation to any pupil at the school, such force as is reasonable in the circumstances for the purpose of preventing the pupil from doing (or continuing to do) any of the following, namely:

(a) Committing any offence

(b) Causing personal injury to, or damage to the property of, any person (including the pupil himself), or

(c) Engaging in any behaviour prejudicial to the maintenance of good order and discipline at the school or among its pupils, whether that behaviour occurs during a teaching session or otherwise.

There are three questions staff need to ask themselves before they consider restraining a child.

1   Could the situation be managed without intervening physically?

2   Is restraint in the best interests of the child? (If the child is restrained/held, will the situation deteriorate?)

3   Is the amount of force being used the minimum necessary and 'proportionate to both the behaviour of the individual ... and the nature of the harm they might cause'? (DfES *Guidance for Restrictive Physical Interventions* July, 1992)

The DfES (1992) also states that 'good practice must always be concerned with *assessing and minimising risk* to children, service users, staff and others and *pre-planning responses* where possible.' In practice this requires the school to have in place:

1   policies

2   plans

3   recording systems.

The school Behaviour Policy must include a section on the use of restrictive physical interventions. Members of staff must make sure that they are acting in accordance with this policy.

Plans

Once a pupil has behaved in such a way that staff have had to intervene using physical restraint, the school needs to develop plans agreeing the strategies to be used when a similar situation arises with the child. This plan must be shared with relevant adults, including parents/carers.

The behaviour plan needs to have a balance of proactive strategies, looking at how to reduce the possibility of problems arising, and reactive strategies which enable the adults to 'have the confidence to respond calmly when things do not go according to plan' (Matthews, 1997). The priority is for the adults to respond calmly and keep the situation under control and to ensure that things do not deteriorate.

In a setting such as a nurture group, holding a child may defuse a potential situation; the child is 'contained'. This needs to be shown on the plan. 'If it can be shown that taking proactive steps reduces risk and prevents the person from becoming distressed or aggressive, then this is clearly the appropriate agreed strategy' (Joint RPI guidance July 2002).

All the adults involved with the child including the parents should be consulted when the plan is being developed.

Recording systems

If there are situations where children are held, these incidents need to be recorded. An effective recording system protects the adults involved and the children:

> In best practice settings there is a bound incident book with numbered pages where the initial entries can be made. This entry can make reference to more detailed records, perhaps using pro-forma incident sheets. (Matthews, 1997)

Record keeping

There are four main areas of record keeping for nurture group staff.

1 Nurture group assessments. These will include Boxall Profiles, SDQs, Referral Forms, Parent Questionnaires, Admission Criteria Checklist and IEPs. There may well be other assessments that schools ask for or that individual practitioners find useful.

2 Class-based assessments. These will include assessments such as Foundation Stage Profile, P-Scales, key words, sounds and letter knowledge. Each school will have a range of assessments showing children's levels of achievements and the nurture group staff will need to work with class teachers to ensure that these assessments are kept up-to-date.

3 Other professionals' reports. Nurture group staff will need to keep reports from other professionals involved with the children and share these with the class teachers.

Behaviour Plan

(Adapted from Team Teach examples 2004)

Name:

Triggers (common situations that have led to problems in the past):

Modifications to the environment/routines (What can we do to prevent problems arising):

Preferred de-escalation strategies (What tends to calm things down?):

Distraction	Negotiation	Planned ignoring
Reassurance	Touch	Verbal advice/support
Withdrawal	Choices offered	Other
Involve new person	Reminders of success	
Humour	Withdrawal offered	

Focus of measures	Measures to be employed
Proactive interventions to prevent risks	
Early interventions to manage risks	
Reactive interventions to respond to adverse reactions	

Record of Physical Intervention

Name of child restrained:

Location of physical intervention:

Date:

Time From: To:

Why was physical intervention necessary?

Describe techniques used:

Was physical intervention constant or intermittent?

Names of staff using physical interventions:

Date incident form completed:

Name

Signature

Name

Signature

Name

Signature

Incident reported to:

Signature

Head teacher

Signature

Nurture group policy

Having a policy that outlines how the nurture group will be organized and run is very important. It should mean that operational issues have been thought through so that the potential for problems is minimized. In the Appendix and on the CD-Rom is an example of a nurture group policy that was adapted from *Policy and Operational Guidelines* (Holmes and Boyd, 2001).

A policy should include the following:

Introduction   How and why has the group been set up? Is the group funded permanently or for a set period of time? What is the group called?

Purpose/aim of the nurture group   How will the children and the school benefit from having a nurture group? What will the nurture group provide?

Description   How many children will be in the group and for how long? What will the room be like and how will the nurture group be staffed? How will the group function if nurture group staff are absent?

Non-contact time   How will non-contact time be used and when will it take place?

Outreach work   Who are the teachers and other professionals that nurture group staff will be working with? When and how will outreach take place?

Steering committee   What is the role of the Steering Committee? How often will it meet and what support will it offer the group?

Referral procedure   Who will be involved in referring children and what assessments will be used?

Entry/admission criteria   How will particular children be selected and which assessments will be used that will enable the correct selection to be made?

Review of pupils   How will children's progress be monitored? Who will be informed? How often will staff meet with parents?

Reintegration criteria   How will this be planned? What will happen if reintegration is not considered appropriate?

Parental links   How will nurture group staff develop a relationship with parents and work with them?

The role of the head teacher   What does the head teacher have responsibility for?

The role of the SENCO   How will nurture group staff work with the SENCO?

The role of the nurture group teacher   With regard to day-to-day management of the nurture group, what are the nurture group teacher's responsibilities?

The role of the nurture group assistant   How does the assistant work effectively with the nurture group teacher?

Monitoring and review of provision   How is the nurture group evaluated? Who is this information shared with? How are decisions made about funding?

4   Termly and weekly planning sheets. The Early Learning Goals and the four areas of child development that form the basis of the *Birth to Three Matters* curriculum (A Strong Child, A Competent Learner, A Healthy Child and A Skilful Communicator) are good places to start when planning a curriculum relevant to the needs of the children in the nurture group. These can be found in Appendix 2 and on the CD-Rom (Figs 5.5–5.7).

Key ideas

> An effective system of support for nurture group staff and other adults working with children with emotional and behavioural difficulties in the school will go a long way to alleviating problems that may occur.

> If staff are having to use restrictive physical intervention in the nurture group or around the school, they must ensure that they are acting lawfully and have effective planning and recording systems in place.

> Nurture group staff should work closely with class teachers to ensure that informative records are kept to effectively monitor the child's progress.

> The Early Learning Goals and Birth to Three Matters curriculum give useful starting points for planning a nurture group curriculum that can recreate an environment equivalent to the child's first three years.

Further reading

Hanko, G. (1995) *Special Needs in Ordinary Classrooms. From Staff Support to Staff Development.* 3rd edn. London: David Fulton.

6

Staff Training

> **This chapter covers**
>
> > a brief history of nurture groups
> > key research on the effectiveness of nurture groups
> > accredited training by the Nurture Group Network
> > delivering nurture group training in school
> > a Kaleidoscope nurture group timeline
> > common problems and questions
> > PowerPoint presentations on nurture group principles and practice.

A brief history of nurture groups

Nurture groups were started in London in 1969 by Marjorie Boxall. In 1978, the Warnock Report stated 'Among compensatory measures which may be taken we have been impressed by the "nurture groups" which have been started in a number of primary schools in London for children approaching or over the age of five who are socially and emotionally affected by severe deprivation in early childhood' (Warnock, 1978: 5, 30). Official recognition was also given in the Fish Report, *Educational Opportunities For All* (Fish, 1985). This report argued that 'as an approach with a clear rationale aimed at preventing many difficulties becoming special educational needs, it is to be endorsed' (2.8.23). The DfES paper 'Excellence for All Children: Meeting Special Educational Needs' (1997) stressed the need for schools to identify children with emotional and behavioural needs and intervene early, and cited nurture groups in Enfield as examples of good practice.

In 1999 the DfEE in collaboration with the Home Office and the Department of Health issued *Social Inclusion: Pupil Support* (DfEE, 1999) which drew attention to the effective work carried out by nurture groups in Enfield. 'The special small classes provide a structured and predictable environment in which children can begin to trust adults and to learn' (p. 11).

Key research on the effectiveness of nurture groups

Alongside these official endorsements the Nurture Group Network has been working in partnership with Cambridge University on a research project to promote primary age nurture groups. Preliminary research findings were published in the *British Journal of Special Education* (Vol. 28, 4 December 2001) and stated that 'in the short term nurture group placement appears to have a positive effect on a significant proportion of pupils ... nurture groups are perceived to have wider benefits to the schools where they are located ... nurture groups offer something far more substantial and enriching than a pleasant environment.'

Glasgow City Council also published research in February 2007 on nurture groups set up in Glasgow schools. The summary *Findings of Current Evaluations* (p. 4) states that 'The evaluation findings totally endorse the Nurture Group approach as an extremely effective intervention strategy to identify and address additional support needs, which fall into the category of social, emotional and/or behavioural difficulties.'

Accredited training by the Nurture Group Network

Nurture groups are based on a well established model which has a strong theoretical framework and which is underpinned by an increasing body of research. It is important that the practitioners have an understanding of this context so that they are able to work confidently within the Boxall model. The Nurture Group Network offers nationally accredited training in partnership with the universities of Cambridge, Leicester and London. The Network also delivers training to local authorities across the United Kingdom. The courses introduce the key themes underpinning nurture groups and include:

- theoretical background

- nurture group organization and management

- understanding children

- research

- using the Boxall Profile Handbook.

The courses are relevant to anyone who is working in or supporting a nurture group.

Delivering nurture group training in school

To support the successful development of a new nurture group the whole school will need an understanding of nurture group principles and practice, both at the start of the group and throughout the life of the project. It will probably fall to the nurture group staff to take a leading part in this training and this can be a daunting task for many people. So this chapter is about providing ideas and resources for running training sessions. Practitioners will be able to adapt these resources to their own settings as required.

The themes for training sessions will include:

•   Nurture group principles and attachment theory: the role of the primary caregiver

•   What is a nurture group?

•   Using the Boxall Profile and other assessments

•   Strategic planning model/steering group

•   The six principles of nurture groups

•   What affects behaviour in school?

The training sessions can be found on the CD-Rom and are in the form of PowerPoint presentations. They can be used as they are or can be adapted to an individual setting. The slides are accompanied by explanatory notes, and sample slides follow in this chapter.

The aim of the training is to share information and develop understanding in the following areas that are central to running a nurture group.

1   The philosophy and theories that underpin the work of nurture groups: this will include developing understanding of principles of attachment theory, attunement, containment, how the brain is affected by trauma in early life and how the adults develop relationships with the children so that change can be effected.

2   Day-to-day running of the nurture group: what would a typical day look like? What is the balance between academic and nurture activities? How is behaviour managed? How do we work effectively with parents and other professionals? How do we manage reintegration?

3   Management of the nurture group: a new nurture group will have an impact on the school and will challenge existing practice. There will be changes. This process needs to be managed to ensure that staff are on board. A strategic planning model is a useful tool to give structure to the discussions that will lead to a clear vision for the school and a means of evaluating the group.

The PowerPoint presentations (on the CD-Rom) have explanatory notes for each talk that make each presentation self-contained. The slides can be printed off from the CD with the explanatory notes, which may be helpful for practitioners preparing to give training. To print, open the PowerPoint presentation on the CD-Rom, go to 'File', 'Print', and select 'Notes Pages' from the 'Print What?' dropdown.

Planning in-school training talks

- Planning and preparation are crucial. Rehearse and practice what you are going to say. Write notes for yourself and don't forget to refer to them when speaking.

- Go through the talk with someone else to see if it works and that you are able to put over the right information clearly.

- Include examples from your own practice. Don't be afraid to talk about what went wrong as well as your successes.

- Relate the theory to real events and/or people, but remember issues of confidentiality. It may not be appropriate to use children's or adults' names in some training settings.

- Ensure that you have agreed the purpose/aim of the training with the member of staff responsible.

- Arrive early and set up equipment so that you are ready to start on time.

- Finish on time.

- Ask someone you trust for honest feedback, so that you can reflect on how the training went and any changes that you need to make before the next time.

- Be aware of your audience. Understand where they are with their knowledge so that you know at what level to start.

- Think about how you can allow opportunities for questions and comments so that there is good interaction between you and your audience.

The Kaleidoscope setting-up process

The following timetable gives an outline of the stages we went though in setting up Kaleidoscope nurture group, which can be helpful when training staff new to nurture groups. This process is not prescriptive and each school will approach setting up a nurture group according to their own situation. However, many of these stages will be common to all schools.

Throughout this process and once the group has been set up and is running, there will be issues and concerns that continue to arise, such as how to use the Boxall Profile, how to manage behaviour or how to build a relationship with a particular child. These and many other concerns will require advice and input from the nurture group staff, and it may well be appropriate to offer regular staff training as a way of developing understanding and expertise within the school community.

Timetable of nurture group development

Find out about nurture groups. Read relevant books/articles/talk to nurture group practitioners/visit other nurture groups/contact Nurture Group Network.

Use Boxall Profile Handbook to inform current practice. Try adopting nurture practice in your current situation. For example, a particular child may benefit from being met by the same adults in the same place and starting each day with a breakfast.

Discuss the possibility of a nurture group with the school's senior management team to see how well it fits in with the school improvement plan.

Reach agreement that the school would benefit from having a nurture group.

Get funding agreed. This may be from the school's own budget, from LEA or it may need to be sourced from elsewhere. The Nurture Group Network is a good starting place to get ideas for funding sources.

Appoint staff. At least one member of staff to attend NGN Certificate course.

Carry out whole school INSET day on nurture groups. Invite speakers form Nurture Group Network or other nurture group practitioners. Key staff to visit other nurture groups. Join Nurture Group Network. Inform your LEA.

Develop steering group. Use the Strategic Planning Model to plan the development of the nurture group. Involve other professionals in this process. Get a wide range of experience on your side.

Inform parents about this new initiative. Send out information leaflets and hold information sessions during the day and evening. Have an information stand in the school on Parents Evening.

Buy resources and fit out a room. Visit other nurture groups and use their ideas.

Plan curriculum/everyday activities and develop nurture group timetable. Be clear about behaviour management.

Select children according to your selection process. This needs to be transparent and understood by school staff and parents.

Start with a small group and gradually add children as confidence grows. Ensure that there is a good mix of children. Set the group up to succeed.

Common problems and questions

'Is the nurture group just for naughty children?'

Parents, teachers and governors need information to enable them to understand the work of a nurture group. Offer information meetings for parents at different times of the day. Have an information stand at Parents' Evenings. Produce an information leaflet for parents. Talk to individual parents or members of staff who ask this sort of question. Use parents who are very supportive to talk to others. Encourage stories of success. Enlist the support of the PTA to help buy equipment for the nurture group.

'The nurture group rewards naughty behaviour'

This is similar to the concern outlined above. Give information to parents and staff. Meet with individuals to hear their concerns and share nurture group principles with them.

Teachers want the difficult children to be in the nurture group for the whole day

It can become quite easy for nurture group staff to agree to have some difficult children in the nurture group for the whole day. This can be seen to be supporting the class teachers at difficult times, such as home time and registration. However, it is important to keep in mind that these children are members of mainstream classes, and it is the responsibility of the class teachers and the nurture group staff to work together to develop strategies to support children at difficult times so that they can still be part of their class. This may involve using Classroom Assistants or nurture group staff coming to the class to support the teacher and the child. What is important is that if a child loses contact with their class because they come to the nurture group straight away in the morning and go home from there, then reintegration becomes much harder because the class teacher has no relationship with them.

'How does reintegration work?'

This can be one of the most difficult aspects of the nurture group work to get right. It will be likely that many of the children who have spent time in the nurture group will continue to require some adult support to enable them to function successfully in the mainstream class. Careful planning is required between all the adults involved and the child so that a programme of reintegration can be planned. Children often do well returning to class for structured activities rather than at less structured times. It may be beneficial to put a time limit on the reintegration process, e.g. once it has been agreed that a child is ready to come back to class, then this will happen over an agreed two- or four-week period.

'Do nurture group staff need non-contact time?'

It is important that nurture group staff are given time to meet parents and other professionals and to carry out assessments. It is very beneficial to do these together, as the input of two adults involved with a child is much more valuable than single input.

'If a member of nurture group staff is absent, does the nurture group still run?'

If the nurture group teacher is absent, the group could shut and the assistant can support the children in their classes. Alternatively, if one member of staff is absent, then the other member of staff can run a reduced group, depending on the type of children. However, there should always be two members of staff working with a group. Individuals should not be left in vulnerable situations with children who are difficult to manage. To help with this, there can also be another member of staff who is the trained person to be used if a member of nurture group staff is absent.

'How do you balance the demands of the National Curriculum and nurturing activities?'

Nurture groups work with children who have emotional and behavioural difficulties and find it difficult to function in their classes. The adults' job is to form a relationship with the children so that children develop a positive view of themselves and their ability to regulate their responses to stress. However, nurture groups are an in-school provision and academic learning is required. Becoming more successful at a range of skills, such as reading, writing, spelling and numeracy can also play a significant part in helping the children develop a more positive self-view. The nurture group staff will have to develop a timetable to give a balance of activities. There are a range of resources available, such as *Curriculum Guidance for the Foundation Stage* and *Birth to Three Matters*.

It is important to remember that nurture groups are addressing 'the basic and essential learning experiences normally gained in the first three years and so enable children to participate fully in the mainstream class' (Boxall, 2002). The OFSTED Report from the first year of Kaleidoscope states, 'Although the pupils are withdrawn from class and are clearly not currently receiving full access to the curriculum, the work of the unit is an important step in promoting the social skills and understanding of these pupils so that they can be fully integrated back into the usual classroom situation working alongside their peers. The work of the unit is therefore very strongly promoting the future educational inclusion of pupils' (OFSTED Report, Christ Church C of E First School, 1999).

'What about differentiation?'

There will be children of different ages and abilities in the nurture group. It is important that the children work at their own level of ability so that they maintain basic reading, writing and numeracy skills. However, there is also much benefit in the group working together. This group time is an opportunity to practise skills such as turn taking, being able to wait, developing eye contact, speaking in a group, being able to listen, being able to develop and practise strategies that enable them to manage difficulties more positively. Doing activities together also creates the nurturing, family feel that is essential to nurture group work.

'Understanding nurture group practice and principles'

Nurture group staff need to ensure that school staff are supported in their understanding of nurture group practice. This will involve running or contributing to staff training. There can be 'Open Days' or 'Open Weeks' when staff can be invited to visit. Information and articles can be photocopied and given to staff. It is important that new members of staff are able to visit the nurture group and see how it works. There can be regular 'nurture group' slots in staff meetings. There will also need to be communication with class teachers who have children in the nurture group.

At the end of the first three years of running Kaleidoscope, the nurture group staff made a DVD showing interviews with staff, parents and other professionals involved with the nurture group about the benefits to the school of having a nurture group. This has been a useful resource and has been shown to parents and staff to help give a deeper understanding of the work of the nurture group.

'How do we approach parents of children who we think should be in the nurture group?'

The class teacher should make initial contact with the parents and begin to raise the possibility of the child attending the nurture group. The parent can then be invited to meet and talk with nurture group staff. They can also be invited to visit the nurture group and see it working. There should be leaflets available for parents to take home and read. There could also be opportunities to meet parents of children currently in the nurture group so that they can feel reassured about its work.

Key ideas

> Nurture groups are based on a well-established model which has a strong theoretical framework and which is underpinned by an increasing body of research. It is important that practitioners have an understanding of this context so that they are able to work with confidence.

> The Nurture Group Network offers nationally accredited training in partnership with the universities of Cambridge, Leicester and London. It is well worth schools sending practitioners on this training, as this will help to ensure that the nurture group is run as well as it can be.

> Also included in this chapter is a timeline showing the stages that we went through when setting up Kaleidoscope as well as the types of questions and problems that arise from time to time.

> Nurture group practitioners may well be called upon to give talks about different aspects of nurture group work. This can be a daunting task, so this chapter and the CD-Rom give six PowerPoint presentations covering different aspects of running a nurture group.

Sample slides from PowerPoint presentation:
Nurture group principles and attachment theory

For the full presentation and accompanying notes see the CD-Rom.

Slide 1

> **Nurture Group Principles
> and Attachment Theory**
>
> **The Role of the Primary Care Giver**

Slide 2

Overview

- "Nurture groups are an in-school resource for children whose emotional, social, behavioural and formal learning needs cannot be met in the mainstream class…
- "Typically, such children have grown up in circumstances of stress and adversity sufficiently severe to limit or disturb the nurturing process of the earliest years…
- "To varying extents they are without the basic and essential learning that normally from birth is bound into a close and trusting relationship with an attentive and responsive parent."

(Marjorie Boxall 2002)

This screen describes what nurture groups are and makes two key points about the types of child who would benefit from nurture group placement. It is important to emphasize that nurture groups are a specific intervention for particular children described above. It is not just for children who are difficult to manage in the class. Marjorie Boxall makes the point that schools make assumptions about children, that they have had the right kinds of experiences that mean that they will be able to function well at school, but these assumptions are not always correct for these children. This is why nurture groups are needed!

Slide 3

What do we need to understand about these children?

- Behaviour difficulties come, in large part, from poorly adapted responses "to the resolution of unconscious conflict" (Harry Ayres et al 1995) as opposed to children whose behaviour difficulties have been learnt (the behavioural perspective)
- "The children's difficulties seem related to the stage in the earliest years when nurturing care was critically impaired."

(Marjorie Boxall 2002)

The work of nurture groups is based on the psychodynamic perspective, where behaviour problems are understood to originate in the unconscious part of the mind. These children's minds are in a state of turmoil, and much of their energy is taken up with this turmoil rather than with being able to learn in the classroom. These children often seem to respond to stress and adversity in ways that are self-defeating. Their responses are often difficult for adults around them to understand and often lead to further difficulties. Situations often seem to arise where the adults want to ask 'Why?'

Slide 4

The importance of attachment

- "There is a critical time in very early infancy when babies form a bond with their primary care giver. This bond is called attachment …"
- "Attachment is observable when the baby behaves in a way which is designed to bring the primary care-giver to them … reaching out, running towards, clinging etc. These behaviours are called *attachment behaviours*."
- "The aim of attachment behaviour is to seek the presence of the attachment figure" to calm anxiety/distress.

(Harry Ayres et al 2000)

Nurture group practice is based on building positive and affirming attachments with the children. Through these attachments, how the children perceive and understand themselves changes. They view themselves more positively. They develop a clearer understanding of themselves and they are more able to regulate their responses to stressful situations.

Sample slides from PowerPoint presentation: What is a nurture group?

For the full presentation and accompanying notes see the CD-Rom.

Slide 1

> ### What Is a Nurture Group?
>
> What Would You Expect to See Happening
> During the Day?

Slide 2

> ### Background to Nurture Groups
>
> - Nurture Groups were originally devised by Marjorie Boxall, Principal Educational Psychologist in Hackney.
> - She recognised that there were an increasing number of children who were displaying a range of emotional and behavioural difficulties that meant that they were in danger of exclusion.
> - Marjorie Boxall understood many of the children's difficulties arose because of gaps in their pre-school development.

Nurture groups were started in Hackney in the 1970s. By the end of this decade, there were around 50 nurture groups. Their further development was disrupted by the break-up of the Inner London Education Authority.

Slide 3

> ### Key Principles…
>
> - Marjorie Boxall decided that if these children were unable to adjust to life at school then it was necessary to ensure that school adjusted to them and the idea of Nurture Groups began.
> - "This child is behaving as a 3, 2, 1 year old, in some cases even younger. I will be for him/her and do for him/her as I would for a child of my own at that age."
>   (Marjorie Boxall 2000)

Having a nurture group allows the school to react flexibly towards children who find it difficult to fit in to the mainstream classes. Schools can intervene early and enable children to reach their full potential over a period of time.

Slide 4

> ### Which Children…?
>
> - The children who were targeted for this support had evidence of deprivation or disruption in their early childhood, e.g.
> - Neglect
> - Sudden loss or violence
> - Relationship breakdown
> - Moving home frequently
> - Drugs or alcohol
> - Chaotic family life

Nurture groups are a specific intervention for particular children whose difficulties can be assessed as linked to the quality of attachment to their primary caregiver. The children will demonstrate real difficulty in managing at school. They may be more withdrawn than others, or much less able to regulate their behaviour. Many of these children will be operating at a very early developmental stage. 'Their experience is limited, poorly organised and has little coherence, and their concepts are imperfect and their feelings confused. They are without a sufficiently organised and coherent past experience.' (Marjorie Boxall, 2002)

Sample slides from PowerPoint presentation:
The six principles of nurture groups

For the full presentation and accompanying notes see the CD-Rom.

Slide 1

> The Six Principles of Nurture Groups

Slide 2

> ### Children's Learning is Understood Developmentally
>
> - Would we do this with a two year old?
> - "The child is a 3, 2, 1 year old, in some cases even younger. I will be for him and do for him as I would for my own child at that age." (Marjorie Boxall 2002)
> - "The healing process must happen with the earliest parent–child … affective sequences… This would include playful movement, touch and family cradling experiences."
>
> (Caroline Archer 2003)

The nurture group should be offering pre-school experiences to the children. Many of their difficulties arise from gaps in early nurturing during the first few years. This is where the 'healing process' begins. It is pre-national curriculum. The *Birth to Three Matters* guidelines are very helpful. The criteria of 'A Strong Child, A Healthy Child, A Skilful Communicator and A Competent Learner' are a good place to start for nurture group practitioners.

Slide 3

> ### The Classroom Offers a Safe Base
>
> - Adults need to adopt an attitude of empathy, love, acceptance, curiosity and playfulness.
> - Guidelines for effective discipline
> 1. Stay physically close
> 2. Make choices for the child and structure their activities
> 3. Set and maintain your emotional tone, not the child's
> 4. Accept thoughts, feelings and behaviours of the child
> 5. Provide natural and logical consequences for behaviours
> 6. Be predictable in attitude, less predictable in your consequences
> 7. Re-attunement following crises
> 8. Be directive and firm, but also attuned to the affect of the child
> 9. Greatly limit the child's ability to hurt you either emotionally or physically.
> (Adapted from Dan Hughes, 'Building the Bonds of Attachment', 1998)

It is absolutely vital that the nurture group is a safe base from which the children can begin to explore themselves and the world around them. Much of this comes from routines and structure of the day: same people, same places, same times. However, what is also of vital importance is the adults' attitude to the children, and their ability to manage the children with firmness, confidence and empathy. Dan Hughes' guidelines are extremely useful in this regard.

Slide 4

> ### The Importance of the Nurture Group for Self-esteem
>
> - Containment
> - For the adults to be able to feel the distress of the child and reflect it back in a way in which the child can manage
> - Containing is not passive, but it involves both partners in an active relationship
> - Strategies for managing/ regulating themselves … so they can say "Well done" to themselves throughout the day

Many of the children in the nurture group find it difficult to regulate their responses to situations that they find difficult. This can happen frequently at school, in their relationships with adults and peers as well as when working. A key role for the adults in the nurture group is to be able to act as a 'mental container' for the children's feelings, where they 'hold' the children's feelings and reflect them back in a way that they can manage. It is also very important for the adults and the children to develop strategies that the child can use independently so that they can begin to regulate themselves in stressful situations. If the child is able to manage themselves they can begin to say 'Well done' to themselves throughout the day and feel positive about what they have achieved.
Initial dependence on the adult eventually leads to child independence.

Sample slides from PowerPoint presentation: Using the Boxall Profile

For the full presentation and accompanying notes see the CD-Rom.

Slide 1

> ### Using The Boxall Profile Handbook
>
> • What is The Boxall Profile Handbook and why use it?
> • The structure of the Boxall Profile
> • When would you use it?
> • What might a typical Boxall Profile reveal?
> • How can you use the information?

Slide 2

> ### What is the Boxall Profile Handbook and Why Use it?
>
> • "The Boxall Profile provides a framework for the structured observations of children in the classroom."
> • It was developed by Marjorie Boxall and colleagues in the 1970s and 80s to support the work of Nurture Groups.
> • Its purpose was to provide a means of assessing the areas of difficulty of severely disadvantaged and deprived children
> • "Confronted with a child whose anxiety-provoking behaviour seems to make no sense, the Profile is where you start. It gives insights and suggests points of entry into the child's world." (Boxall Profile Handbook 1998)

These slides should be used in conjunction with Chapter 3, Assessing Which Children Belong in a Nurture Group and Working with them. You would need photocopies of the Boxall Profile histograms and the reports that come from completed Boxall Profiles as well as photocopies of Dan Hughes' Guidelines on Facilitating Effective Discipline and Facilitating the Capacity for Fun and Love. The reports and the Dan Hughes Guidelines would need to be used on the final slide.

Slide 3

> ### Empathy
>
> • "Empathy, that ability to begin to see the world through the eyes of the child's experience is an important component in any approach's success. Empathy provides the adult with the question that needs to be asked continuously when working with the child with EBD: "Why do I think this child behaved in this way and what does it mean for the approach I use?" It provides the basis upon which the pupil can begin to feel valued and understood … it provides an understanding as to why the EBD has occurred."
>
> (John Visser 2002)

The Boxall Profile is the main assessment tool used in nurture groups. It does not give answers or tell the practitioners what to do, but rather allows the practitioners to gain an insight into the child's world and begin to get a fuller understanding of how the child has been affected by their earlier experiences.

Slide 4

> ### The Structure of the Boxall Profile
>
> • The Profile is in two sections
>
> • Section 1, Developmental Strands, consists of items which describe different aspects of the developmental process of the pre-school years. Satisfactory completion of this first stage of learning is essential if children are to make good use of their educational opportunities (Boxall 1998).
> • The first cluster reflects how the child is engaging with the world.
> • The second cluster reflects levels of personal development and awareness of others.

The first section of the Boxall Profile is made up of two clusters, Organization of Experience and Internalization of Controls. The first cluster is concerned with how the child relates to the world, how they engage with people around them and how well they are able to make connections between experiences that they have. The second cluster is concerned with the child's personal development, how secure they are, how well they managing a group and how well they regulate their responses to difficult situations. An 'average' child will have high scores in this part of the Profile, whereas nurture group children will have low scores in many of the columns.

Sample slides from PowerPoint presentation:
A strategic planning model

For the full presentation and accompanying notes see the CD-Rom.

Slide 1

A Strategic Planning Model

• A Framework for the Steering Group
• How To Manage Change

Slide 2

What is Strategic Planning

- Strategic Planning provides a technique for establishing and maintaining a sense of direction.
- The emphasis is on responding proactively rather than reactively to change
- "Strategy is the process by which members of the organisation envision its future and develop the necessary procedures to achieve that future." (Weindling 1996)

Starting a Nurture Group will bring about many changes to a school. These changes will include
- how adults in the school understand children
- how adults will respond to children with emotional and behavioural difficulties
- Developing new knowledge and understanding about attachment theory
- Working with parents
- Working with other professionals
- Ensuring that the Nurture Group is integrated into the whole school
- Training on Nurture Group Principles and practice
- Supporting the Nurture Group staff

It is vital that these and other changes are managed. If a Nurture Group is just started up without the necessary planning, it is very likely that it will not succeed, or that it will be very difficult to get the whole school staff being clear about what the Nurture Group actually is.

This Strategic Planning Model is simply a process that enables key discussions to take place to clarify the Vision and Aims and Values of the Nurture Group so that the whole school can have a good understanding.

Slide 3

Why Bother With Strategic Planning?

- "Caring is not enough. Changing is not enough. Spending money is not enough. Raising standards is not enough. In fact, each of the single-issue quick fixes imposed on education might be failing for the wrong reasons … We have been selecting means (hows) before agreeing on the ends. It is now time to get ends and means related. Being strategic is knowing what to achieve, being able to justify the direction, and then finding the best ways to get there."

(Kaufman 1992)

A school can just start up a nurture group up and hope for the best, or it can give some time to thinking and planning, which will ensure that fewer problems will occur over the life of the Group and that there is greater clarity about what a nurture group is and what its aims are.

Slide 4

Issues/Areas for Development

- Whole school integration
- Role of teacher
- Selection of children
- Involvement of parents
- Other professionals/other schools

Whole school integration: Shared values and understanding of all staff, development of Nurture Group policies, Mission Statement,how to show success/evaluation, staff knowledge/training, staff support, behaviour management, new staff

Role of Teacher: day-to-day planning/organization, curriculum development, record keeping, contact with class teachers, reintegration, staff training/INSET, working with parents, working with other professionals and other schools, working with assistant, staff support, OFSTED school's self-evaluation form

Selection of children: development of transparent admission criteria, reintegration process, working with other teachers and other professionals, composition of Group

Involvement of parents: informal and formal meetings, involvement of outside agencies, sharing assessments, reviewing progress
Other professionals: training other schools, other staff/professionals to visit, advising, training with other Nurture Group staff, Nurture Group Network, LEA involvement

Sample slides from PowerPoint presentation: What affects behaviour in schools?

For the full presentation and accompanying notes see the CD-Rom.

Slide 1

> ## What Affects Behaviour in Schools?
>
> A Nurture Perspective

The basis for much of this presentation is Heather Geddes' excellent book, *Attachment in the Classroom* (Worth 2006).

Slide 2

> ### What is the problem in schools?
>
> - There appear to be an increasing number of children who find school very difficult.
> - These children do not seem to be able to respond to normal, everyday rewards and sanctions systems that schools have in place.
> - These children are increasingly harder to understand and manage and often leave the teacher feeling "eroded and fragmented" (Boxall 2002).

Slide 3

> - "School is based on the assumption that children are essentially biddable, will be willing to entrust themselves to the teacher … have an awareness of how the world around them functions, are sufficiently organised to attend and follow through what is required … school thus continues a learning process which began years before in the home. These assumptions are not necessarily true for severely deprived and disadvantaged children."
>
>   (Boxall 2000)

Slide 4

> ### Risk Factors
>
> - Low self-esteem
> - Homelessness
> - Illness
> - Poverty
> - Poor housing
> - Parents with relationship problems
> - Physical, emotional or sexual abuse.
> - Alcohol/drugs
> - Bereavement

Appendix 1

This appendix contains completed examples of sample documents which appear in Chapter 2.

Vision

For everyone to know the value of the nurture group, to support its aims and values and for the funding to continue

For people to know success stories

For there to be clear, quantifiable success criteria

For there to be an impact on mainstream education and there to be a change in practice and provision

Other schools in the area to learn from the nurture group and be empowered

For people to recognize that there is a need for this type of provision

For the nurture group to be an integral part of the local federation of schools

For parents to see the nurture group as essential

To be viewed by other professionals as being an important way of reaching families

The school to hold it in high esteem

Happier children and teachers

Children see the nurture group as just part of the school

It is an established resource

There is less school exclusion

Values Audit

Personal beliefs

An essential part of the education system in the twenty-first century

An important early intervention strategy

Preventative provision – not just containing the problem

Nurturing approach applicable to whole school

Adherence to well researched principles rather than cultural values

Monitoring and assessment tools used to establish transparent entry and exit criteria

Reintegration seen as important right from the start of a child's placement

Difference from mainstream classes

Flexibility

Slower pace

Homely environment

Freedom to use different approaches

Pursue individual needs of children

Opportunity to play

Filling gaps in children's education

Use of food

Smaller number of children

What would you want to see in a nurture group?

Play, learning and having fun

Talking

EBD concerns being met

Activities matched to the needs of the children

Children being taught how to play

What would you want to hear teachers say about the nurture group?

The nurture group has developed my skills

I know what to do with the children when they are back in class

There are people I can talk to and get support from when I am faced with a child I find difficult

I feel relief that this child isn't in a failing situation any more

I understand the nurture group principles

What would you want to hear the children saying?

I feel happy, safe and valued

I feel that I am being helped

I can do my work

I know more about myself

What would you want to hear the parents say about the nurture group?

My child is more confident

I know why my child is in the nurture group

This is a good provision

I know what is going on

I can take part

Staff see my point of view and I don't feel blamed

I know where the provision is leading

My child is happy

I can see all the children in the school benefit

I understand that this provision is supportive

I feel involved

The nurture group has helped my child at home

My parenting skills have been helped

Mission statement

Who are we: what is our identity?

The nurture group provides a flexible and preventative resource that is responsive to the needs of particular children attending the school. Within the nurture group there is a secure and reliable environment for children showing signs of emotional stress and behavioural difficulties. The nurture group enables children to re-experience pre-school nurture from caring adults who work actively towards the children's successful reintegration into mainstream classes.

Nurture group staff work in partnership with class teachers, assistants and parents to enable consistency of approach, both at home and at school. Links are being developed between schools in the Federation and other professional organisations such as Social Services so that the nurture group's philosophy and approach can be developed.

What are the basic social needs we exist to fulfil?

The nurture group is part of a continuum of provision offered by the school. It enables the school to meet the needs of those pupils who have evidence of gaps in pre-school development leading to emotional, linguistic and intellectual deprivation, making their chance of success at school very slim. The school recognizes that some children are unable to adjust to life at school and it is necessary that the school adjust to them by providing this type of provision.

Children who are targeted for the support offered by the nurture group are those who have evidence of severely deprived early childhoods. The principle underlying this provision is that the child will be responded to at whatever developmental stage they are presently at.

What do we want to do to recognize and respond to these needs?

Placement within the nurture group will be considered for children who are under-achieving for social, emotional or behavioural reasons. The children will be considered against the Entry Criteria Checklist. The Goodman's Strengths and Difficulties Questionnaire and the Boxall Profile will be used to objectively assess children's needs and their suitability for placement in the nurture group.

Parental agreement is necessary. All referrals will be made in consultation with parents on a standard form. Nurture group staff will meet informally with parents and will also arrange more formal parent interviews to discuss children's progress. Reintegration to mainstream class will be planned with the child and all key adults. Each child will be monitored and reviewed on an ongoing basis. Consultations with the Educational Psychologist and other professionals will be arranged as appropriate.

There will be a maximum of 12 children in the nurture group at any one time. Children will attend for a period of up to four terms.

How should we respond to our key stakeholders?

A Steering Group has been set up to enable an agreed vision to be formulated. The Steering Group will meet twice a year to ensure that the needs of key stakeholders are being addressed in the context of staying true to the nurture group philosophy. Action Plans will be drawn up and reviewed at each Steering Group meeting to ensure that the shared vision for the nurture group is being achieved.

What is our philosophy and our core values?

School is based on the assumption that children are essentially biddable and willing to entrust themselves to the teacher and have some understanding of their expectations. School presupposes that children have an awareness of how the world around them functions and they are sufficiently organized to be able to cope in large group situations. Schools believe that they are continuing a learning process that began in the home. However, these assumptions are not necessarily justified in the case of severely deprived and disadvantaged children.

The problems of such children are understood as stemming from the lack of early care and support in families suffering severe social fragmentation and stress. The child does not experience the reliable sequence of events that enable them to make sense of the world around them. Trust in adults is weakened because the level of support that the child gets does not reliably meet his needs.

A nurture group creates an environment where children can make up for missed early experiences. Within the nurture group, there is recognition that some children are functioning at a much younger developmental age, and they find it difficult to function in a busy classroom. A nurture group day is slow moving, with clear structure, routine and much repetition. Management of behaviour is consistent and fair.

Appendix 2

Nurture Group Policy

Introduction

The school has been able to appoint an additional teacher and a full-time assistant to work with small groups of children who will benefit from being in a smaller group and in a less formal environment than the normal classroom can provide.

1. Purpose/aim of the Nurture Group

- To provide a flexible and preventative resource which is responsive to the particular needs of the children attending the school.

- To provide ongoing assessment and support for children showing signs of emotional stress and behavioural difficulties with the aim of enabling the child to access the curriculum and participate fully in school life.

- To provide a secure and reliable environment where children can learn by re-experiencing pre-school nurture from caring adults who actively work towards their successful integration into their mainstream class.

- To help children to learn to behave appropriately, use their curiosity constructively, improve their self-esteem and develop confidence through close and trusting relationships with adults.

- To work in partnership with class teachers and parents to enable consistency of approach, both at home and at school.

2. Description

- Nurture Groups are a unique, preventative resource based on well documented psychological theory and research.

- The Nurture Group is based in a separate room with a home-like area and an area set aside for formal learning.

- Children will attend for a maximum period of up to four terms.

- There will be a maximum of 10–12 children in the Nurture Group at any one time.

- The children will be on the register of their mainstream class and they will join their class for appropriate activities.

- The children will spend lunchtime and playtime with other children in the school. Some children may need extra support at these times.

- The Nurture Group will consist of a full-time experienced teacher and a full-time assistant who will work as a team. Neither adult will be available to cover for absent staff within the school.

- In the absence of the Nurture Group Teacher it will not be possible for the group to function; therefore the children will return to their mainstream classes and be supported by the Nurture Group Assistant and other Key Adults. If the Nurture Group Assistant is absent, the Nurture Group will continue with the Teacher and a trained Classroom Assistant.

3. Non-contact time

Non-contact time will be required for the Nurture Group team to

- See parents

- Attend case conferences

- Keep records

- Carry out observations

- Meet with other professionals

- Liaise with other school staff

- Attend INSET

Non-contact time is on ....

4. Outreach work

The Nurture Group will continue to build on existing multi-agency outreach work. Training, advice and support for colleagues in the local area will be offered. Nurture Group staff will develop links with other professionals as appropriate and work with them to enable the child and the family to be offered an effective package of support.

5. Steering Committee

The Steering Committee will meet for one full day to enable a cohesive and agreed vision to be formulated. This will be achieved through working through a variety of activities including a Values Audit, a Stakeholder Analysis and developing a mission statement

The Steering Committee will meet twice yearly to ensure that progress is being made towards achieving the vision and to offer guidance and support as required.

6. Referral procedures

- All referrals will be made in consultation with parents on a standard form.

- Formal assessment by an Educational Psychologist is not a pre-requisite for admission, but consultation and discussion of relevant factors may be necessary.

- All referrals will be discussed with the Head Teacher, Class Teacher and Nurture Group Team.

- A variety of assessment procedures will be used to inform referrals. These will include the Goodman's Strengths and Difficulties Questionnaire, the Boxall Profile and appropriate academic assessments.

- Parents will be kept fully informed about the outcomes of these assessments and meetings.

7. Entry/admission criteria

- Parental agreement is necessary

Nurture Group placement will be considered for children who are underachieving for social, emotional or behavioural reasons. This will include:

- Children who are very restless, cannot listen, behave impulsively or aggressively

- Children who are withdrawn and unresponsive and who have difficulty relating to others

- Children whose known history suggests that they may be at risk.

- The Goodman's Strengths and Difficulties Questionnaire and the Boxall Profile will be used to objectively assess children's needs and their suitability for placement in the Nurture Group.

8. Arrangements for review of pupils

- Each child will be monitored and reviewed on an ongoing basis. Consultations with the Educational Psychologist and other professionals will be arranged as appropriate.

- Formal reviews with parents will take place on a termly basis.

9. Reintegration/exit criteria

- Reintegration will be planned with the Head Teacher, parents, Class Teacher, Nurture Group team and other Key Adults consulting with the School Educational Psychologist where appropriate.

- Where reintegration is not considered appropriate an alternative action plan will be agreed. This may involve assessment at the next stage of the Code of Practice.

- For more detail please refer to the Reintegration Policy.

10. Parental links

- All children attending the Nurture Group require resources beyond those usually provided by the school. The school will work in partnership with parents. This will be achieved through formal reviews each term and more frequent informal discussions concerning the progress of the children.

- The Head Teacher will be responsible for dealing with any complaints from parents. Complaints which remain unresolved will be referred through the school's normal procedures.

11. Role of the Head Teacher

The Head Teacher has overall responsibility for the functioning of the Nurture Group within the school. The Head Teacher is responsible for:

- The operational management of the Nurture Group

- Management of Nurture Group staff as members of the school community

- Oversight of curriculum planning and monitoring of work

- Ensuring that the Nurture Group Teacher participates in the school's appraisal procedure

- Ensuring Health and Safety procedures are followed in accordance with the school's policy

- Ensuring that the Nurture Group operates within the guidelines of the LEA's policy on equal opportunities and the school's SEN policy.

12. Role of the School SENCO

To liaise with the Nurture Group team. This will include the development and implementation of IEPs; to be involved in formal reviews as required; to support curriculum development; to be involved with selection and reintegration.

13. Role of the Nurture Group Teacher

The Nurture Group Teacher is responsible for the day-to-day management of the group. The teacher has the following duties:

- To maintain the Nurture Group principle – this is to provide a carefully routined day where there is a balance of learning and teaching, affection and structure within a home-like atmosphere.

- To organize and plan the activities and curriculum of the classroom, bearing in mind the needs of the children.

- To keep records of individual children's progress.

- To coordinate the work of the Nurture Group assistant

- To liaise with other professionals when appropriate

- To actively work in partnership with parents in the development of their children.

- To help children manage successfully in less structured sessions including playtimes.

- To participate in INSET within school and the Frome Federation

- To coordinate Steering Committee meetings

- To carry out and contribute to school policies and procedures.

14. Role of the Nurture Group Assistant

The Nurture Group Assistant works in partnership with the Teacher. This role is to assist the Teacher in necessary tasks, including planning, and to participate in appropriate INSET.

15. Monitoring and review of provision

- The Nurture Group will be evaluated through OFSTED inspection.

- The Nurture Group Steering Committee will meet to ensure the Nurture Group principle is being maintained. It will also monitor the success of the provision and provide support and guidance.

Nurture Group Topic Planning

Term.......................

Early learning goals	Week beginning	Week beginning	Week beginning	Week beginning	Week beginning	Week beginning	Week beginning	Week beginning
Personal and social development *A strong child* *A healthy child*								
Language and literacy *A skilful communicator* *A competent learner*								
Mathematics *A competent learner*								
Knowledge and under-standing of the world *A competent learner*								
Physical development *A healthy child* *A strong child*								
Creative development *A competent learner*								

Rotating Activity Planner – Nurture Group

Term.................. Week beginning..................

Date	Small world	Fine manipulative	Puzzles	Construction	Technology	Imaginative play	Hall	Whole group sessions	Topic work	Sand, water, malleable, tactile
Monday										
Tuesday										
Wednesday										
Thursday										
Friday										

Strong child   Skilful communicator   Competent learner   Healthy child

Nurture group learning objectives

Term......................................

Learning objectives

Resources

Assessment opportunities

Glossary

Amygdala   Part of the limbic system that plays a major part in processing emotions and storing emotional memories

Attachment   A two-way relationship that is formed between an infant and their primary caregiver. Secure attachment occurs where the primary caregiver is able to respond appropriately to the needs of the infant. An insecure attachment can develop when the primary caregiver is not emotionally available to the infant over a significant period of time

Attunement   A two-way, shared, positive, emotional relationship between caregiver and infant, focused on facial expression, gestures and voice

Behaviourism   The theory that a person's behaviour is determined by what they have learned. This means that inappropriate behaviour can be unlearned and more positive behaviour can then be learned

Brainstem   The most primitive part of the brain that governs basic functions such as breathing

Cerebral cortex (neo-cortex)   The part of the brain that processes what the senses perceive, and where conscious decisions are made

Consultation   An opportunity to think together and clarify issues about particular children or situations and resolve problems

Containment   The process of 'holding' another person's emotions and reflecting them back in a safe, reassuring and manageable way, to help them learn to manage their own emotions and feelings

Dyadic   A two-way relationship between an infant and the carer

EBD   Emotional and behavioural difficulties

Empathy   Seeing the world through another's eyes; getting in touch with their thoughts and feelings

Eternal verities   A set of beliefs, values and ideas that underpin successful approaches to working with children with EBD regardless of the setting

Inner speech   The ability to talk to ourselves to aid processing of thoughts

Inner working model   A image of oneself that determines behaviour; secure attachment allows a child to develop a positive image of itself as a worthwhile individual

Limbic system   The emotional centres of the brain, where the brain started to be able to learn, remember and to adapt

Projection   A defence mechanism whereby a person unconsciously vents unwanted feelings through what they do or say, onto someone else, in the belief that they are the cause of the bad feeling

Self-regulation   The process of understanding and managing feelings and emotions, and responses to stressful situations

Stakeholder   A person who can affect or be affected by a project

References

Allen, B. and Matthews, G. (2004) *Team-Teach Intermediate Tutors Manual, Version 1.* East Sussex: Steaming Publishing.

Archer, C. and Burnell, A. (eds) (2003) *Trauma, Attachment and Family Permanence: Fear Can Stop You Loving.* London: Jessica Kingsley.

Ayres, H., Clarke, D. and Murray, A. (2000) *Perspectives on Behaviour: A Practical Guide to Effective Interventions for Teachers.* 2nd edn. London: David Fulton.

Bennathan, M. and Boxall, M. (1998) *The Boxall Profile, Handbook for Teachers.* Maidstone: Nurture Group Network.

Bennathan, M. and Boxall, M. (2000) *Effective Intervention in Primary Schools. Nurture Groups.* 2nd edn. London: David Fulton.

Boxall, M. (2002) *Nurture Groups in Schools. Principles and Practice.* London: Paul Chapman.

Craig, P. (2005) 'Selfish altruism', *SEBDA News,* 7: 26–7.

Department for Education and Employment (DfEE) (1999) Social Inclusion: Pupil Support. Circular 11/99. DfEE Publications.

Department for Education and Skills (DfES) (1992) *Guidance for Restrictive Physical Interventions.* Crown Copyright. DfES Publications.

Department for Education and Skills (DfES) (1997) *Excellence for All Children: Meeting Special Educational Needs.* Green Paper.

Department for Education and Skills (DfES) (2001) *Principles and Policies of the SEN Code of Practice.* Crown Copyright. DfES Publications.

Fish (1985) *Educational Opportunities for All* (The Fish Report). London: ILED.

Geddes, H. (2006) *Attachment in the Classroom: The Links Between Children's Early Experience, Emotional Well Being and Performance in School.* London: Worth.

Goldberg, S. (2000) *Attachment and Development.* London: Arnold.

Goleman, D. (1996) *Emotional Intelligence: Why It Can Matter More Than IQ.* London: Bloomsbury.

Goodman, R. (1999) Strengths and Difficulties Questionnaire. www.sdqinfo.com

Goodman, R. (2007) personal communication.

Greenhalgh, P. (1994) *Emotional Growth and Learning.* London: Routledge.

Hanko, G. (1995) *Special Needs in Ordinary Classrooms: From Staff Support to Staff Development.* 3rd edn. London: David Fulton.

Hinshelwood, R.D. (1999) 'Countertransference and the therapeutic relationship: recent Kleinian developments in technique'. Paper available online at www.psych-matters.com.

Holmes, E. and Boyd, E. (2001) 'Policy and Operational Guidelines'. Unpublished nurture group policy, London Borough of Enfield.

Hughes, D. (1998) *Building the Bonds of Attachment: Awakening Love in Deeply Troubled Children.* London: Jason Aronson.

Hughes, D. (2000) 'Dyadic, Integrative Parenting with Traumatised, Attachment Resistant Children', Notes from lecture tour.

Kapalka, G.M. (2005) 'Avoiding Repetitions Reduces ADHD Children's Management Problems in the Classroom', *Emotional and Behavioural Difficulties* 10(4): 264–79.

Kaufman, R. (1992) *Mapping Educational Success: Strategic Thinking and Planning for School Administrators.* Newbury Park, CA.: Corwin Press.

Long, R. and Fogell, J. (1999) *Supporting Pupils with Emotional Difficulties: Creating a Caring Environment for All.* London: David Fulton.

Meichenbaum, D. (1975) *Cognitive Behaviour Modification.* New York: Plenum.

Ofsted (2000) *Evaluating Educational Inclusion: Guidance for Inspectors and Schools.* Office for Standards in Education, Crown Copyright.

Shuttleworth, J., Miller, L. and Rustin, M. (1997) *Closely Observed Infants.* London: Duckworth.

Visser, J. (2002) 'The David Wills Lecture 2001: Eternal verities: the strongest links', *Emotional and Behavioural Difficulties* 7(2): 68–84.

Warnock (1978) *Special Education Needs* (The Warnock Report), Cmnd 7212, London: HMSO.

Weindling, D. (1996) *Understanding School Management. Module 2: Managing School Effectiveness.* Course E834, Unit 6, Strategies for development. Milton Keynes: Open University.

Useful Websites

www.educationpsychologist.co.uk

www.nurturegroups.org

www.sdqinfo.org

www.Team-Teach.co.uk

www.Steaming-training.co.uk

Index

Note: References marked 'P' are to full page photocopiable resources

Th   tur   b